ECCLESIA MYSTERIA

FIRST EDITION

ECCLESIA MYSTERIA

© Martinet Press 2015

martinet.press@safe-mail.net

ISBN-13: 978-0692432082

ISBN-10: 0692432086

Cover art courtesy of Steven Lilley,
via Flikr under Creative Commons license.
www.flickr.com/photos/sk8geek/3300937037

For the Credentes:

In hoc signo vinces

FOREWORD

This book, titled *Ecclesia Mysteria*, is intended to lay the foundation for a new spiritual community or congregation, which our tradition calls the Ecclesia. The Ecclesia can best be described as a contemporary spiritual congregation that remains faithful to the original Gnostic tradition of the Classical Sethian movement. Gnosticism is path of spiritual practice, rather than spiritual dogma. Adherents (called Credentes) choose to embrace Gnosticism because they want to experience revelation, rather than to blindly believe. Like many of the world's great mystery traditions, Gnosticism holds that we live in spiritually vibrant cosmos, which is inherently good and magical, though not entirely safe or without danger. The Ecclesia is a guide or path which leads its travelers on a journey of revelation. It is genuinely amoral in that we do not concern ourselves with moral codes or concepts, which change from decade to decade, but rather we focus on eternal things which cannot and do not change. These are the only things that really matter, and that should matter.

This book is intended to fulfill three purposes:

1. It offers a Gnostic mythos that is both traditional and progressive. That is to say, it makes use of existing classical gnostic texts as a foundation, but provides a new reading of

those classical texts which is truer to the original antinomian spirit of those works.

2. It offers the reader a series of **solo** practices that can be put into practice immediately. These are (by design) familiar to anyone from a Catholic or liturgical background, but with an interpretation that is genuinely Gnostic and Logos-centered in orientation.

3. It will provide steps for those who wish to go beyond and join an actual community of Gnostics.

This book has been written for people curious about Gnosticism, for those currently practicing some Gnostic tradition, and also for those Credentes who already belong to the Ecclesia and who would like to have a single volume with codifies our primary practices. Whatever your reason for reading this book, I would like to offer you my hopes and prayers that you find something of benefit in this text.

May the grace and power of our Lord be with you always.

Your servant,

✠ **TAU CONSTANTINE**

TABLE OF CONTENTS

ECCLESIA MYSTERIA

SACRED TRADITION

ECCLESIA MYSTERIA

ECCLESIA MYSTERIA: AN INTRODUCTION

GNOSTIC SPIRITUALITY is unique, in that it offers its initiates a genuine religious tradition that is authentic, established, but flexible. Gnosis – or sacred knowledge – is already within us. It's not some external gift or dark secret that we can read in books. Consider this: through science, we know that all the stars and planets in the cosmos originated with the "Big Bang". That means that we ourselves are the very stuff of stars – we are pure cosmic light which has been somehow made into solid, living bodies. When you think about it, it is truly incredible. So everything in the cosmos is already a part of us, and no external force can give you something that isn't already within you, at least not on a material or spiritual level. Gnosticism, then, is a spiritual science that allows us to explore the inner mysteries, because the human is held to be sacred and a microcosm of the cosmos itself. Gnostics reject the idea that the universe is bad or corrupt, or that people are innately wicked or bad (though we acknowledge that people can do bad things) because Gnosticism sees the entire cosmos as sacred in origin and worthy of respect and care. This is in stark contrast to the major religions of today, which desperately try to reach an imagined and external deity, hoping that it will save them from the world. By contrast, Gnostics love the world, delight in living life to its fullest, free of guilt and shame. Gnostic tradition holds that by understanding and genuinely knowing yourself, you can come to know the amazing and terrifying being that is within each and every one of us. We are *not* gods, but we have the potential to enjoy life with an awakened sense of our divine origins.

Gnosticism recognizes a paradox: on the one hand, since we are presently human, the supreme reality is utterly beyond our ability to comprehend with our senses and intellect. On the other hand, our salvation (from our spiritual adversaries) absolutely requires that we obtain genuine and direct knowledge of this supreme reality. So being finite ourselves, we must use finite tools and finite words to try to express infinity and an infinite creator. Terrifying! But with patience, hope, and faith, we are capable of remarkable spiritual evolution. And this is not merely a 20th century expression for self-improvement, but genuine evolution where the human evolves into something more than human, something genuinely preternatural.

One of the greatest gifts of Gnostic tradition is that it provides us with a set of mental or spiritual tools with which to practice divine psychology. Here, we do not mean *medical* psychology, but refer to the original meaning of the word. *Psyche*, being Greek for "soul", and *logy*, from "logia", meaning the discourse or science. So *psychology* is the science of the soul. In Gnostic tradition we

12

do not see the soul as diseased, but instead consider it to be an expression or expansion of the original divine person, which is why Gnosticism is and always has been an inward-glancing tradition: the divine light (*psyche*) is inside already inside us.

Unlike other many faith systems, especially modern or recently developed systems, Gnosticism does not claim to be easy. At its very fundamental levels, certainly, anyone can undertake the outer forms of Gnostic practice, and equally anyone can put their faith in the *traditio sacra* (sacred tradition) and *mysterium* (the divine secret). But this alone does not necessarily lead to direct encounter of the divine presence. Genuine gnosis requires self-sacrifice – not in the Christian sense of "giving till it hurts", but sacrifice of the Self. To make genuine progress along the path, one must be willingly to surrender one's self entirely to the Aeon, and that is a frightening thing. Genuine spiritual transformation can cause mental, psychological, and even physical suffering – and for many, this is necessary. This is not to say that it does not equally provoke ecstasy and joy! But the path can be challenging. Equally for this reason, Christ founded the Ecclesia so that a community would exist to give guidance and support on the journey to encountering the Ultimate Reality.

GNOSTICISM holds that all existence and all entities are expressions (or *emanations*) of a single primordial being. This being is eternal, perfect, and encompasses literally every facet of existence. Most Gnostics agree on this common doctrine, though they have differing names for the Supreme Being. In the Ecclesia Mysteria, we follow the tradition of those who call this being "Abraxas". Of course, a supreme being is nameless by nature, but as we ourselves are limited beings, it is normal and even necessary to give names to the unnamable. Gnosticism differs from other traditions in that Abraxas is not an eminent, distant, or separate being, but rather it is understood as an immanent force that sustains all of existence. Scientists can detect a *dark matter* in nature that appears to be present in all matter, yet operates independently from any of the known laws of physics. We suspect, in our tradition, that this is an evidence of the presence of this primordial being. So Gnosticism holds that the divine presence is not an externalized presence that we need to reach out to, but rather that it is an immanent within every living being. Indeed, Abraxas is the energy that flows throughout the cosmos – in a sense, the cosmos is the visible emanation of the power that originates from Abraxas. As with other of the world's wisdom traditions, Gnosticism teaches that the Supreme Being is the only self-sustaining and independent reality. Every spirit, creature, galaxy and moment in the cosmos is dependent for its being on Abraxas or one of its emanations.

Here is a mystery: in eternity past, Abraxas coiled within the great Void (Grk. κένωμα). The Void was pure, in that it was empty of all limitation and being, except for Abraxas, which was undifferentiated from the Void. Some gnostic teachers referred to this Supreme Being or place as the "Deep Waters" (Grk. βυθός), the Divine Void, and recognized Abraxas as the very sentience or awareness the Void. The Void was empty not in the sense of incompleteness, but empty in terms of differentiation – that is to say that Nothing existed, that is, the Void, without qualifier or separating principle. As the Holy Scriptures report in the first chapter of Genesis, the Void was neither formless nor void, and in our limited and finite way of thinking, we imagine it to have been like an infinite ocean of liquid darkness. We do not mean *darkness* in the mundane sense of "an absence of light", but rather the true Darkness as described in the Gnostic scriptures, which is mysterious, silent, and impenetrable. This is not chaos (though it was called chaos by some philosophers), but rather the primal state of eternity and unity. The Void could be considered as the very 'body' or essence of Abraxas, if such terms could be applied to an infinite and eternal being. In an attempt to personify Abraxas, early cultures sometimes depicted Him as a monstrous composite entity, often draconic or serpentine in nature. In reality (or more appropriately, outside of it), these mythological images are understood to suggest that Abraxas is beyond any

15

conventional description, as an infinite being is without limit and therefore characteristic.

Now as Void moved around its master, Abraxas emanated a new being, which Gnostic tradition sometimes calls *Barberlo*, the Holy Spirit and Divine Mother. As Abraxas was the very spirit of the Void, Barberlo was the spirit of the Abraxas. Barberlo is the first aeon and emanation of Abraxas and has Her divine essence from Him. Barberlo was perfect from Her origin and an inconceivably powerful spirit, though finite in that She has a source, and while She is a source herself, She herself does not exist independently. Just as Abraxas is the essence of eternity and infinity, Barberlo is the essence of generation and creative impulses of the primordial Void.

Now for reasons that Gnostic tradition does not explain, within the heart of the Void, in the deeps of time Abraxas chose to produce a storm of terrible light, the bight-shining Pleroma. As the Holy Scriptures record, the Supreme Being begins creation with a great shout: *Let there be Light* (Genesis 1:3). Mechanically, we understand that the Darkness converged and drew it on itself, growing denser and denser, just as coal condenses to become a diamond, which comes from coal but is not itself coal. Then, like a diamond exposed to even greater pressures, this primordial density exploded – there was light: the Pleroma appeared with a mighty roar, and became the divine throne and city of Abraxas, shining with colorless fire. Beyond the divine light of Pleroma was still the dark silence of the Void – which changed not, and cannot ever change, as it is eternal. Just as the Void is the absence of any matter or limitation, the Pleroma was the absolute essence of potential, the raw and unabated firestorm of unending creation.

Desiring to create and expand, which is Her perfect nature, Barberlo meditated on the colorless flame of Pleroma, which is the gift of Abraxas. Then by His consent – which was the first *gnosis* – She emanated the Logos, the Divine Son. The Logos is the communicative impulse of Abraxas and Barberlo, the essence of discourse and speech and meaning. The urge of the Logos is to know and be known, and to lead others towards knowing. Thus the Holy Trinity dwelled within the Pleroma, and the Pleroma seethed and resonated eternally within the Void. Lord, Lady, and Logos (or Wyrm, Wyrd, and Word) were in perfect harmony and unity.

Then Abraxas repeated: *Let there be Light*, and the Logos then emanated four other aeons, who in turn each emanated successive aeons each in outward cascading succession. These beings are those which humanity names "deities" or "gods", ascribing to them the creation of the world and the worship and reverence which is not their just due. The aeons themselves are born of the light of Pleroma, and so they themselves are creative and generative by nature. In turn, they created

17

the holy archons, which humanity call "angels" and "spirits". These are the spirits which assist the aeons, and while they (like the aeons) are born of Pleroma's light, they are of lesser order and power. And all these were in the beginning obedient to the Logos. Thus as the Holy Scriptures say, *all things that have been made were made through the agency of the Logos, and without the Logos the Void would have remained silent and untouched* (Gospel of John 1:3). Thus the divine Void (κένωμα) was filled with increasing light, as each aeon expanded outward and upward from its generating aeon. And as the Pleroma grew outward over the Great Void with the aeons multiplying and pushing outwards into the emptiness, a third realm formed as a barrier between them. This was the Cosmos, the world of creation. Where Pleroma is infinitely ever-changing, and the Void is infinitely changeless, the Cosmos by nature is finite and subject to cycles and laws of nature. Where the Pleroma seeks to expand and grow, the Void seeks to consume and dissolve all into its limitless depths. Thus all things in the Cosmos experience birth, growth, stagnation, and dissolution, only again to find rebirth. But at the beginning the Cosmos was rough and unshaped, without beauty or shape, and as the Holy Scriptures say, it was rough and disordered (Genesis 1:2). For this reason also the Holy Scriptures place the Heavenly Aeons (Pleroma) above the Cosmos, but the Great Void is beneath the Cosmos.

So the Nameless God is the ultimate source of all realms and worlds, but the Cosmos itself was fashioned and shaped by the aeons that descended from the Holy Trinity. And each of the aeons and archons had great knowledge and power, each according to the store of light with which they were themselves created. Now to each of the planets and galaxies was assigned an aeon or archon, to oversee the turning of the heavenly bodies. These are the guardians of the Cosmos, who define the laws of nature and growth and evolution. To our world, Gnostic tradition tells that there was assigned a great archon, whose name is unknown but is referred to by the Jewish Scriptures as the *Elohim*, sometimes called the *Demiurge* ('craftsman') in the Greek texts. Now where the other worlds nearby are mute and silent, our world was blessed with life. So the Elohim was tasked with the protection and care of those first living beings, for which reason he is justly called Lord and Father and God by those that dwell on Terra, for indeed Christ calls him *the God of this World*, and the Demiurge asserts his authority to appoint the rulers and deputies of our nations and states, which he reminds Christ during the temptation (Matt. 4: 8-9 *"All these things I will give You if You will fall down and worship me."*)

At first the Elohim was content with this task, for he was both wise and exceedingly learned in the mysteries of the material cosmos, and so he accepted to care for our world with diligence. Yet over the millennia, he became arrogant on account of the Holy Light with which he executed his functions, and he forgot that his authority and power were his by loan from the aeons above him (and not his by right). Then rather than teaching and caring for creatures and the lower spirits, he began instead to dominate them, demanding to be called Lord rather than acknowledging the aeons higher than him. Now the animals which the Demiurge created were noble but simple, having only that power which is necessary for animation, and the Demiurge desired not to be a caretaker but rather to be served and worshiped. So he fashioned from the earth a man and woman and breathed into them a portion of his own share of the divine Light. And so the man (Adam) and woman (Eve) were made, hybrids of the mortal world and the spiritual realm. So the flesh is of the Cosmos, which is noble, but the spirit is of the Pleroma, and both are ultimately of the Void. For this reason humanity struggles sometimes to reconcile its dual nature, where it desires the pleasures of the physical realm, but also longs uneasily for ethereal things that are beyond the natural senses.

Now rather than cherishing and teaching humanity, the Demiurge attempted to maintain them in ignorance of their divine heritage within the false paradise of Eden, where they were meant to be kept as tenders of beasts. Declaring himself to be the one and only deity, he commanded them to worship him as their lord and creator; and he commanded those spirits (lesser and greater) of

Terra to acknowledge his reign, and he began to act in defiance of the higher aeons.

But his defiance was not unmarked, and having created humanity with the divine spark, he had gone beyond his own authority. So the Holy Logos descended in the form of the Serpent, and taught Adam and Eve the first gnosis through the consumption of the apple of knowledge, which was the first sacramental act, saying (Gen. 3: 4-5): *You will not certainly die, for the Creator knows that when you eat from it your eyes will be opened, and you will be like the Creator, knowing good and evil.* And indeed, this moment is considered by several spiritual traditions to have been spiritually transformative for the human race. The demiurgic religions, which are dependent on shame and guilt to control people, try to explain this moment as the beginning of some manner of innate or original sin. But Gnostic tradition instead explains this moment as a beautiful and sanctifying experience in which Eve and Adam were awakened and became (as the Serpent promises) like the Archons in terms of understanding. Thus humanity slipped free of the greatest snare of the Demiurge, which is *Ignorance.*

Now once the first humans experienced this first taste of gnosis through the Serpent's actions, it was impossible for the Demiurge to take it away. For true gnosis comes from a realm above the authority and station of the Elohim, and further,

21

such aeons as time and destiny do not allow a thing to be undone once it has been allowed to cause to happen. So the Demiurge took on physical shape and attempted the seduction Eve. But being awakened by the gnosis through the salvific actions of the Serpent-Logos, Eve caused her reflection to take on autonomy as a simulacrum, and the incarnate Demiurge had relations with this animate construct instead, and the twins Cain and Abel were born from this union. Adam and Eve later produced Seth, who was the firstborn of the other children that came from their newly awakened gnosis. Seth was the first human to be born of gnosis, and was held by many early Gnostics to be the Serpent Logos, who had descended again to continue the salvation of humanity. In any case, Gnostic tradition holds that humanity today is descended from Seth and his unnamed siblings.

Now the Demiurge is ancient and exceedingly cunning, and Terra is his kingdom by gift of the aeons. Further, having shaped the bones and sinews of humanity, he knows well the weaknesses and vulnerabilities of the mortal mind and heart. Thus he devised a new snare: *Religion.* Descending from his spiritual realm over Terra, he appeared to select men and declared himself to be the chief of all deities and powers. To those humans who accepted him as their lord and master, he showed favor and increased them in strength and stature of body and minds. Biblical tradition states that the

Elohim revealed himself to Noah and Abraham, promising them many children if they would serve as his messenger. Then later to Moses he bestowed great magical power – for indeed, the Demiurge has great power, and the spiritual secrets of Terra are his to share and to teach when he so wishes.

However, when the Demiurge tried to establish his priesthood through Moses, the children of Abraham rebelled against his monotheistic claims and refused to give up their cult of the other archons that lay claim to Terra. For while the Demiurge is the greatest among the archons of Terra, he is not the sole archon here, and other archons (which we call *gods*, or *devas*, or *elemental beings*) desire worship and adulation. So in anger, the Demiurge struck the children of Abraham with a terrible plague of serpents, thinking to slay them in the desert. Yet again the Serpent-Logos interceded, causing Its divine image to be shaped by Moses so that Its spirit could be presenced within Terra, even if only briefly. So the Torah reads (Numbers 21:9): *And Moses made a bronze serpent and set it on the standard; and it came about, that if a serpent bit any man, when he looked to the bronze serpent, he lived.* And the children of Abraham came to revere the image and worship it, to the extent that it was latter shattered by jealous disciples of the Demiurge (2 Kings 18:4).

Now over the centuries, the Demiurge crafted Religion such that it made people to feel shame and humiliation over the very material needs and instincts that the Demiurge himself had placed within them.   Human nature is by nature expansive – so greed becomes prohibited; where it is competitive, pride becomes sinful; since humans require sex for reproduction, so lust becomes shameful. Moreover, Religion expressly forbid the spiritual sciences by which humanity might reach out and contact other Archons and Aeons – namely witchcraft, necromancy, and magic. In this way, the Demiurge sought to keep humanity dependent upon him entirely for supernatural protection from the elements, and from the other more bestial and dangerous of the spiritual predators that lurk in the dark places of the world.

Despite the original gnosis of Eve and Adam, Humanity's fate would have been unending slavery to the Demiurge and his archons. However Abraxas does not suffer challengers to His supremacy, and nothing has happened or can happen without His knowledge, for He is the only true deity.   So again, the Serpent-Logos descending into the human sphere, this time being willingly to be incarnated into the flesh of a man and be born, subject to all the hardships of Terra.   Thus the Serpent-Logos became Christ Jesus, and came among us to teach us of His divine Father and Mother.

Now prior to the incarnation of the Serpent-Logos, all demiurgic religion had been largely Terracentric and had no thought for the life after death, teaching that mortal life ends without hope of rebirth – and this is so that the Demiurge could take captive the ignorant and guilty souls of humanity for his own delight and sport. But the Christ taught humanity that there is a world beyond Terra, and that all humans have a share in the Divine Pleroma (or Heaven) and can achieve rebirth there and not be trapped within this sphere. More importantly, the Christ taught the sacraments, which are those simple rituals by which we are able to come into direct contact with the highest aeons, even Barberlo and Abraxas themselves. These sacraments Christ gave to his most trusted of students, charging them to spread his teachings to all corners of the globe. This new community, he said, would be the Ecclesia (church), and the forces of the Demiurge would not be able to overcome it. Indeed, the Ecclesia is the Bride of the Christ, and he taught that when the End of Days should come, that the Ecclesia should be brought back into Perfect Communion with Abraxas. So indeed while the Ecclesia at present is based on Terra, the politics and economics and wars of this world are not the primary concern of the Gnostic. Rather, these things are the snares of the Demiurge, which distract humans from their first and inescapable loyalty – which is to Abraxas, which coils eternally at the heart of the Void. The Lord Christ said (Matthew 10:16): "*Be shrewd as serpents but innocent as doves*", meaning that the Gnostic initiate should understand beware the various traps of the Demiurge, while not falling prey to them.

Let us be clear: Gnosticism does not teach that the world is corrupt, or that matter is somehow to be disregarded. It is true that some Gnostic groups began to teach such confused doctrines, but these groups were acknowledged as semi-Catholic traditions, and were mixing demiurgic beliefs with authentic Christ-inspired teachings. The Serpent-Logos (as Christ) taught that we should celebrate the material world, because it is a genuine and holy emanation from the spiritual world. In fact, the Cosmos itself is an Aeon, and the Demiurge of Terra is considered to be planetary archon in a vast galaxy of equally great archons. So we do not revile the material world, and indeed we seek to enjoy the pleasures of the flesh just as Christ did Himself. We know that the Christ enjoyed food, alcohol, friendship with his students and friends, and it is generally acknowledged today that he had romantic relationships (outside of marriage) with several of his female students, such as Mary Magdalene. We believe that Christ was genuinely amoral when it came to the religious values of his day, and as our Ecclesia takes Him as our holy exemplar, we encourage our devotees to engage in similar pursuits with a good conscious.

After his brief teaching ministry, the Christ withdraw from the mortal sphere to return to Pleroma. However, as his disciples begged him for support and aid, and as the Christ is genuinely enamored of the Ecclesia, he agreed to send his Mother, the Holy Spirit. Thus She descended at Pentacost and marked the faithful (*Credentes*) with the colorless flames of the spirit. The Gnostic tradition believes that through the sacrament of Baptism and Anointing, the initiate of the Mysteries can receive the presence of the Holy Spirit, which thereafter possesses and empowers the initiate so long as Its holy presence is maintained and revered. Thus the font of gnosis is both the innate divine light of humanity, but also the presence of the Holy Spirit which further guides and protects the initiate from the hostile demiurgic forces.

Of course, the Demiurge has worked tirelessly to establish it's selfish and malignant religions in all corners of the world, yet Gnosticism teaches that the Logos has descended in various times and places to counter the lies of the false god. And thus various faiths and spiritual systems have evolved over the course of human evolution, each offering to put humanity at the feet of the gods as slaves and worshippers. Uniquely, Gnosticism offers to set humanity free of its shackles, and to lead our souls away from the shackles of delusion, choosing rather to seek Unity with the Supreme Reality of the Void. There, Christ taught, through the dissolution of our mortal selves and our false egos, we can be clothed with power and immortality, and "*we shall know as we are known*" (I Cor. 13:12).

Indeed, *"His dream,"* as one modern saint has said *"is of the day when all shall be inside him and all that says 'I' can say it only through him."* So this is our hope: that one day we shall all be inside him, and that (together with the Logos and Holy Spirit) we shall say "I" together through Him, and Him alone.

THE ECCLESIA

The Gnostic tradition began over 2000 years ago, and it is very well documented. Gnostic churches and mystics and saints flourished for several centuries, though the Catholic Church perceived the self-centered gnostic revelations as a threat to their domination of spiritual life, and so they instigated hostilities that eventually drove Gnostic tradition underground. But Gnosticism survived well into the medieval period, which we can see in the beliefs of the Cathars and certain Sufi sects. In fact, in the modern period, Gnosticism has faced a revival, fuelled partially by the discovery of many Gnostic manuscripts that were hidden for centuries. The Gnostic Church is an eternal tradition, and while sometimes it has operated in secret, it cannot die because its teachings are genuinely holy, transgressive, and transformative.

The Gnostic Church was founded by the Divine Logos, which is the divine interlocutor. This being has intervened repeatedly in human history in different guises, to save and to educate humanity about its divine origins. Within our specific tradition, the first recorded appearance of the Logos was in the Garden of Eden, when it descended in the form of the Serpent of Light to give knowledge (gnosis) to Eve and Adam. It appeared millennia later in the person of Christ, who was a great mystic and teacher. Christ taught the techniques and rituals by which gnosis can be obtained, and laid the foundation for the movement that became the Gnostic Church. Of course, the early Gnostics had different branches and different understandings of Christ's teachings, and so Gnosticism was never a monolithic tradition, but a multifaceted and loosely aligned series of societies and communities that shared a common conviction and dedication to the Holy Trinity (Father, Mother, Son).

Early Gnosticism looked very similar to Christianity, as they shared a similar founder and similar practices and a common sense of Messianic tradition. However, our tradition holds that the hostile and selfish forces of the Demiurge infiltrated the early Messianic tradition and perverted its teachings. Where Gnosticism remained true to Christ's teachings that humanity deserves freedom and joy, the Christian Church began to teach that humanity was essentially shameful and weak. As Gnostic leaders taught their followers to be disinterested in the corrupt intrigues of the Roman Empire, the Catholic Bishops allied with the Empire's leaders and enjoined Christian support for the corrupt politics of that day. Where the Christian Church was openly patriarchal and misogynistic, the Gnostic Church taught gender equality and had female and male bishops, priests, and deacons. Christian sexuality was tied to guilt and ritual impurity, whereas Gnostic sexuality has always been celebrated as a sacred and transformative act.

With these things said, it is evident why the Gnostic congregations were so fiercely persecuted by their Catholic cousins. And it should be said clearly: we do not see these movements as purely human initiatives. In every Christian cruelty, in every Catholic inquest and witch-burning, we see the hateful will of the Demiurge and its archons who have tried to put out the eternal light of gnosis. But we take heart, for the Divine Logos taught his beloved disciples that the true Ecclessia can never die, nor can those who put their faith in Him. As the Serpent-Logos says to our Grandmother Eve in the Garden of Eden (Genesis 3:3): *For the Elohim knows that in the day you taste the fruit of knowledge, your eyes will be opened, and you will become divine like Him, knowing good and evil.* Thus we remain hopeful that through tasting the sweetness of gnosis, we will indeed attain the highest reward.

TRADITIO MYSTERIA

The sacred and esoteric tradition of the *Ecclesia Mysteria* is a living and eternal tradition. Articulated partially in the Biblical Gospels, and more perfectly in the Gnostic Gospels, we believe that the sacred tradition is alive, powerful, and pervasive. The Holy Spirit is present on earth, and desires that the tradition should be widespread, albeit in different guises and forms. So Gnosticism can be found in many different places, at diverse times, and under different names. The Gnostic tradition is not a dead or static entity then, or a philosophy which can be learned and discarded. There is, we believe, a definite will and guiding purpose that directs and assists the Gnostic congregations in their efforts to establish themselves and to grow as communities.

Being a spiritual Tradition that stems ultimately from the Void and the Pleroma, and bearing the approval and assent of the Holy Trinity and the holy Aeons, genuine initiation in the Gnostic Ecclesia is considered very necessary for real spiritual evolution. As a consequence, since the appearance of the Gnostic tradition, the Demiurge and his archons have sought to interfere with the movement by perverting its teachings into Catholic (i.e. demiurgic) Christianity, and persecuting those Gnostic centers and saints wherever and whenever possible. So in order to safeguard the validity

Tradition (as the guardian of initiation), in the classical and early medieval period, the Tradition developed an organizational structure that served to vouchsafe the practitioners who claimed to possess gnosis, to see whether or not their gnosis was genuine and indeed coming from the Aeonic (and not demiurgic) sources. As the Tradition developed with time and the Gnostic practices became richer and deeper with experience and practice, certain sacraments were identified as too potent for simple initiates, and were withheld for the priests and bishops of the Gnostic community. As a result, a complex system of ritual consecrations was developed and had to be undertaken before a potential candidate could be given access to some of the more advanced spiritual practices. This particular mode of transmission was referred as "apostolic", after the apostles who carried out the mission of Christ after his ascent into the Pleroma. The apostles were nominated with a simple ceremony in which the disciples of Christ laid their hands on the head and shoulders of the initiate, and prayed that the Holy Spirit would enter into and possess them. These apostles in turn performed the same ceremony of transmission and possession on their own students, in order to raise them to the same "order" as the apostles themselves. These "apostolic" chains of spiritual transmission lasted well into the medieval period, and the last of the authentic Western chains died with the Cathar movement, though the Eastern (or Sufi) transmissions continued unbroken into this century.

However, certain Gnostic congregations today claim to have elders or bishops that have received genuine apostolic consecrations. On the one hand, this indicates a very real and healthy respect for tradition and the heritage of the various gnostic ecclesiae. On the other hand, we must recognize that the current chains of apostolic consecration are a historical re-creation or re-enactment (albeit well-intentioned) of earlier ceremonies, and that none of the current episcopi or bishops possess consecrations that go back more than two or exceptionally three generations. In other words, the current apostolic lineages do not stretch back further than the 20th century – at least if one considers "lineages" that are genuinely gnostic initiations, and not Roma Catholic or quasi-Catholic consecrations, due to their demiurgic nature. Now, this does not imply that those ceremonies have been invalid in terms of the spiritual efficiency or intention, and indeed our Ecclesia does recognize that there are modern gnostic bishops and priests who have received genuine spiritual empowerment and a special gnosis which is unique to the sacerdotal vocation. *However,* if modern Gnostic teachers and leaders are sincere, they will admit that the validity of their sacerdotal gnosis arises from the baptism of fire which comes from the direct intercession of the Holy Spirit, rather than through the hands of a human initiator/initiatrix with a recently revived lineage.

This distinction between initiation via the Holy Spirit and initiation via human hands is important, because the global Gnostic community today is quite small, and there are many people who might wish to join a Gnostic assembly or ecclesia, but feel that they cannot become initiates or partake of the sacraments without being physically present. And here lies again one of the deadliest snares of the Demiurge: religions deceive people so that they feel that they have to be in a specific place or building or even institution in order to be spiritual. Granted, it is very helpful and even necessary within our own tradition to have a small space for daily spiritual practices. But many of the early Gnostics lived lives of quiet isolation and seclusion, choosing to seek the Supreme Aeon in the quiet of the desert, or mountains, or caves. In some cases these pious *Credentes* would remain in contact with a few of their own students, or perhaps with a Bishop, or else form a very small community of likeminded spiritualists that lived apart from society. Further, we teach and believe that it is entirely possible to experience significant spiritual growth in isolation or in private, and more importantly, that since gnosis flows comes from the Aeons, there is no empowerment or consecration that cannot be obtained in private and without a human intermediary. Thus we consider that our sister Gnostic churches of the

21st century are valid and real, but their authenticity comes from the strength of their convictions and dedication to practice, rather than any claims to (impossibly) authentic lineage.

Now that having been said, the Lord Christ, who is the Serpent-Logos, taught that most people in fact require a community for growth and stability, and moreover for teaching and spiritual development. Even the holy saints and mendicants of the classical and medieval periods were not immune from errors, and so we state that the primary role of the Ecclesia is to provide guidance and to help initiates to avoid the potential dangers and errors of the spiritual path. In addition, while potentially an initiate can obtain all empowerments in seclusion, this comes only with tremendous effort and sacrifice. So the Christ taught that part of the role of the Ecclesia is to ease the spiritual journey, by allowing its senior members to transmit some of their gnosis to other candidates. This transmission can exceptionally take place in written word, but more commonly through the performance of certain sacramental rites. While it is not strictly necessary to have a teacher, it is also foolish (even arrogant) to assume that one can unlock the secrets of divine wisdom without a teacher – and history says that those few saints who did so independently undertook severe austerities, which are nigh impossible to replicate today. In short, we encourage all initiates of the mysteries to seek a qualified instructor whenever and wherever possible. And while face-to-face communication is ideal, and necessary for the performance of sacraments, the digital age has made other forms of communication increasingly viable for some types of instruction.

In short, our tradition considers its adherents to be members of the Ecclesia, whether or not they are near a Bishop or Congregation, and whether they study with a mentor, or practice alone and in secret. If someone reads this book and feels called by the Aeons to join our community, we are very glad to have them. Ultimately, we trust in the Holy Spirit to guide those genuine seekers to the gnosis which they need to achieve salvation and Communion.

ECCLESIA MYSTERIA TODAY

The Ecclesia Mysteria began as a closed congregation in the 1990s, by a small group of Credentes based in the United States and Canada. While the Ecclesia has already appreciated the rich diversity of classical Gnostic traditions, it holds itself to be a modern revival of the Sethian denomination of Gnosticism. This means in practical terms that the sacraments and holy texts used by the Ecclesia Mysteria are those used in the Sethian liturgies, as opposed to the Ophites, Basilidians, or Valentinian liturgies – though these other traditions are rightly held in reverence. Our Gnostic congregation seeks to be an authentic vehicle for genuine gnosis, with a strong basis in the classical Gnostic tradition, yet faithful to the spirit of our age. We do not seek to pretend that we live in the same day and culture as our spiritual ancestors who articulated the Gnostic Gospels, yet we do seek to embody their beliefs and convictions in a way that makes sense for the 21st century. The Ecclesia has an administration and a process for those who wish to be recognized as members of its congregation, though it does not charge for congregational membership, or ask for donations, though initiates are expected to contribute towards the costs of their sanctuary (if they attend one) and to support the movement with time or energy as they are able. While Gnostic spirituality has always been loosely organized and more informal than its Catholic counterpart, there are nevertheless two general Modes of organization, and four Orders of initiation. As with the first ecclesiae, Ecclesia Mysteria consider all genders to be equally capable of taking Holy Order if so called by the Holy Spirit.

As such, we sanction and encourage the following two Modes of worship:

THE HERMITAGE: we acknowledge that since the earliest period of the ecclesiae, some initiates lived in seclusion or practiced in secret. We honor and revere those initiates today who choose to follow this example, especially those whose lifestyle and circumstances do not allow them to partake in the sacraments with a larger congregation. This initiate often avoids contact with other Gnostics, or else makes contact rarely, and practices a life of simple sacramental worship. This mode of Gnostic spirituality is referred to as the Hermitage.

An example of the Hermitage would be as follows: *Jessica discovers a copy of* Ecclesia Mysteria *at her local library. She reads it, understands and appreciates some of its Lessons, and begins to practice the Devotions on a daily basis. Once a week, she celebrates the Sacraments. After three months of spiritual practice, she decides to write to the email address at the back of the book. After exchanging a few emails with the administration, she decides to request a mentor. Jessica comes into contact with Shannon, one of the Priests who lives in the same state. She emails Shannon once a month to ask questions or get advice, and occasionally they meet for coffee. Jessica enjoys a spiritual life of meaning and purpose without feeling a desire to meet or celebrate with other initiates. She chooses not to share her spiritual convictions with her friends or family, knowing that Gnosticism would be difficult for people of other faith traditions to understand.*

THE CONGREGATION: we acknowledge that since the earliest period of the ecclesiae, some initiates were fortunate to meet or find other like-minded seekers, and to form a small local congregation referred to as a Congregation. A Congregation is headed ideally by a Priest, who is in turn in contact with a Bishop. In the absence of a Priest, the most senior member of the Congregation serves as Deacon, similar to an acting Priest.

An example of the Congregation would be as follows: *Devon is interested in a female colleague from work. He learns that she is a member of a Gnostic congregation that celebrates the sacraments at a small weekly meeting at the local college. Devon begins to attend the weekly meetings, and reads a copy of* Ecclesia Mysteria. *He begins to perform the Devotions daily, and celebrates the Sacraments weekly with the group. Later, Devon is ordained as a Deacon and assists the Priest with the rites. He later moves to a different city and begins a Congregation there with several new friends who are interested in experiencing the supernatural mysteries. Eventually, Devon is ordained as a Priest, and becomes involved in helping to mentor others who want to learn more about gnosis and Gnosticism. Devon is able to be open with his friends and family about his commitment to the Ecclesia, and lives a life of supernatural wonder and joy.*

It should be stressed that the Ecclesia Mysteria is not an occult society or hermetic fraternity with grades. Rather, each of the Holy Orders is complete in terms of its function and purpose. All humans are called by Abraxas, but few are called to the Sacerdotal orders. The four Holy Orders of Initiation are as follows:

The Credentes: this is the Order of those who have chosen to accept and practice the tradition, after a period of sufficient reflection. A *Credens* has undergone the Rite of Confirmation, and may practice the Mysteries alone (see above: Hermitage) or as part of a congregation (see above: Congregation). The Credens who has practiced faithfully for five years may be called a *Perfectus* (pl. *Perfecti*), which can be used as an honorific. The status of Credens is the foundation of the Ecclesia, and is equivalent to a member of a Catholic congregation who has undergone the rite of Confirmation, and is a permanent commitment to the path. Even if a person may choose to leave the Ecclesia later in life, this Rite leaves an indelible mark on the soul which cannot be removed by any natural force. However, in Gnostic tradition, the Credens (like the later three Orders) has a sacerdotal character, as the initiate is responsible for the celebration of the Sacraments, even in the absence of a Priest.

The Diaconate: this is the second Order of the Ecclesia. Since ancient times, the Deacon has served a two-fold role. First, they serve as the servants and assistants of the Congregation, and assist the Priest and/or Bishop as required. Second, an initiate who is considering Ordination to the Priesthood must serve at least one year as a Deacon, partly to gain liturgical experience, and partly as a period of intense reflection and self-study. The Order of Diaconate need not be a permanent commitment, though tradition states that the charisma (power) of the Logos does not depart even if the initiate requests to be relieved of their commission to the Diaconate.

The Sacerdote: in conformity with the tradition of the first ecclesiae, we hold that all initiates have a sacerdotal character and mandate. However, we likewise confirm the teaching the Lord Christ, who established his disciples and apostles with a special charisma (power) to serve, teach, and lead the Ecclesia. Thus our tradition calls for the anointing and empowering of certain individuals who are entirely dedicated to the cause of the Holy Trinity. A candidate for the Priesthood must be a Credens in good standing for three years, and serve one year as a Deacon before undergoing Ordination. While Priests can live and serve in Hermitage, the Rite of Ordination is not published, and is only shared with actual candidates of the Priesthood. Priests serve mainly to lead a Congregation, to celebrate the Sacraments, and to confirm the gnosis of the Credentes and Deacons as appropriate. The Priesthood is the first of the two sacerdotal Orders.

The Episcopate: in keeping with the holy tradition of the first Gnostic congregations, we recognize that the Ecclesia needs senior initiates who provide leadership and coordination to the Congregations, and even discipline in times of need. Thus Bishops serve to lead their own Congregation, and to oversee the activities of the

Priesthood within their geographical province. Bishops offer guidance and support to other initiates, and assist with the performance and coordination of Ecclesia initiatives. The ordination to Order of the Episcopate confers the highest empowerments that exist within the lineage of our Ecclesia. The Episcopate is the second of the two sacerdotal Orders.

ON OTHER GNOSTIC MOVEMENTS

The last several decades have seen a sudden appearance of several movements which claim to be Gnostic. Some of these are obviously valid expressions of the Gnostic tradition, and have found doctrines rooted in historical practices and texts of the early Gnostic assemblies. Other movements have emerged, without any reference to the historical Gnostic ecclesiae or gospels for their authenticity, which raises questions as to how they define the concept of gnosis and Gnosticism in general. Yet more alarming, several contemporary Gnostic movements have demonstrated a strain of teachings that are clearly demiurgic. This is most often demonstrated in a supposed "holy rejection" of the *hylic* or material world, which is paired with an equally confusing insistence on expensive material altars, sanctuaries, and spell components, none of which is part of the original Gnostic movement. Self-hatred and self-annihilating doctrines are frequently added to the mix, with considerable emphasis on demiurgic

Old Testament traditions, at the expense of the New Testament which conceals the actual gnosis. Any movement or teacher that celebrates self-annihilation is in thrall of the Demiurge, and should be avoided. This is not to say that such movements or teachers, are without their own spiritual power, but the Ecclesia Mysteria holds that the Demiurge seeks to corrupt the authentic gnostic tradition through a counterfeit and impure gnosis, and so vigilance is called for in all circumstances.

This should be made clear: genuine Gnostic tradition celebrates the sacredness of the material world, as a gradual result of the fathomless will of Abraxas. On the one hand, the Serpent Logos taught us to not be overly attached to the material world or even the heavenly aeons, as they are impermanent. The Christ says (Mark 13:31): *Heaven and earth will pass away, but my words will never pass away.* Since the Logos himself descending into the world, and since the Holy Spirit is present indwelling are creatures and objects, we cannot and must not consider the material world to be wicked or defile in essence. If one does mistakenly believe that the Cosmos is genuinely unclean and impure, then one cannot use material objects for spiritual purposes, whether or not they have been "consecrated" – and to think so is to court self-delusion. We hold, rather, that the material world is good and sacred, and we are glad to partake in it. And as long as we are incarnate in this world, we cannot and should not reject it, for the nameless god allowed us to take shape here as an expression of its labyrinthine designs. A practicing Credens seeks to exercise (not *exorcise*) physical, mental, and spiritual urges as expressions of the inviolate will, and will never claim otherwise.

ON SOUL AND SPIRIT

Gnostic tradition depicts the universe as a cosmic battleground of sorts, in which humans are essentially defenseless cattle at the whims of supernatural forces that are sometimes benign, sometimes hostile, and most often indifferent. Religions themselves demand spiritual slavery or slavish adoration of divine powers that bully their adherents, threatening with suffering and damnation if the demands of the abusive and selfish deities are not met. Shame and humiliation are considered normal and even desirable in the face of the supposedly benign deities, who offer to magnanimously forgive humanity for acting in accordance with human nature. Now the shackle, the metaphysical leash around the necks of humanity is the soul – the *psyche* – of which religions make much. The soul is the Demiurge's gift to humanity, and it is responsible for all the feelings of guilt, fear, shame, and inadequacy which humans experience on a daily basis. The psyche provides people with an innate sense of connection to the divine, but this is unfortunately to the way that a dog is connected to its master by means of a leash. Thus the social construct of "good" and "morality" is a spiritual tool of the Demiurge. Morality as humanity understands it is really nothing more than a very sophisticated neurosis. This is not to say that Gnosticism is in favor of evil as opposed to the good, but rather that Gnosticism believes that humanity in its pure state is meant to be amoral, like the pure beasts of the field. Laws and regulations may be necessary, but the complex and neurotic social, political, and legal codes of today are the spider's web in which humanity has become hopelessly entangled. Our personality, our sense of self and our respective obligations is all a construct that flows from the power of the Demiurge. This is not entirely a bad thing – it allows us certain intellectual and esoteric hardware than animals do not have – but our intellect is like an operating system crippled by the spiritual "malware" that is built into it.

Fortunately, there is hope of salvation from this mental and psychic mire. While the Demiurge curses humanity its neurotic soul, Abraxas offers humanity the gift of the Spirit. In the sacred myth of Adam and Eve, by consuming the apple, the proto-parents Adam and Eve each absorb of a sliver of the Abraxian consciousness, which causes them to be aware of the spiritual world and the aeonic forces and currents running through the cosmos. What is vital then to a healthy, functioning Gnostic is the proper balance of the soul and spirit. Clearly, the soul cannot and should not be denigrated, as our ability to even conceive of such a thing stems from the mental hardware of the psyche. However, it is necessary for the soul to be predominant in order for humanity to live in freedom and joy. For this reason, the Serpent-Logos descended to Earth as Christ, taught the Sacraments, Devotions, and Austerities, and then ascended back into the Pleroma – at which point the Holy Spirit was able to descend and to inhabit the students of Christ, empowering them to live genuinely spiritual lives. The Sacraments are very, very powerful tools that allow the grace and potential of the Void to flow upwards and into the hollowness of the human heart, transforming humans into genuinely spiritual creatures. Spiritual, in this context, does not mean "sensitive" or "religious" in the modern sense, but rather that the human has transcended their mortality through partaking in an existence that is eternal. Thus a practicing Gnostic has opened the doors of their heart, and invited the essence of the Supreme Aeon to indwell them and to become part of them.

This gnosis comes at a price: the Gnostic must surrender the psyche to the Void, so that it can be cleansed and transformed. The traditional myth of the mystic "selling their soul to the Devil", is in fact a perverted demiurgic retelling of real salvation. True and genuine salvation, as Christ says, comes through being born again. In John 3:5, Christ says *Very truly I tell you, no one can enter the kingdom of God unless they are born of water (i.e. βυθός) and the Spirit* – in other words, the initiate must offer the psyche as an offering to the Nameless God, and experience rebirth as a creature filled with the Holy Spirit.

What does this mean practically? Tradition states that this sacrifice and rebirth is a difficult and painful process. In some cases, people attempt to cling to their old and sinful self, which greatly complicates the invitation of the Holy Spirit, and can lead to possession by lower elementals or else torment by archontic forces who do not want to lose their hold over the human being. For this reason, we have reports of saints and hermits who were haunted and tortured by demonic visitations. These spiritual torments did not begin until after the saints began to pry themselves free of the demiurgic matrix, and this is a warning to would-be saints today. Gnosis and liberation come at a steep price. However, those who have the courage to perform the Sacraments and Austerities to intake the Holy Spirit will be transformed into new beings. Those initiates who have begun to practice the devotions and austerities often begin to experience strange dreams and surges of intuition. Synchronicity and coincidence become weekly and then daily events, as the gnosis begins to build inside of the Credentes. Increasingly resonance with the Holy Spirit brings powerful states of confidence and courage, and a greater sense of the social and spiritual currents in the Credentes environment.

It is normal for struggles to develop between the psyche and pneuma, especially in the beginning of Gnostic practices. The psyche, being the leash of the archons, may experience moments of panic and wild guilt at the increasingly alien presence of the pneuma. But as the Credentes learn to increasingly invite the indwelling present of the pneuma, the neurotic ravings of the psyche are slowly silenced. The guilt and shame are reduced, the inhibitions are stripped away, and the Credentes slowly undergo a metamorphosis into an archonic being.

ON SPIRITUAL EMPOWERMENT

As the Credentes become increasingly aware of the reservoir of Gnosis building within them, they become aware of the whispering of the *pneuma* (spirit) within them. The *pneuma* becomes the constant companion of the Credentes, offering guidance and wisdom. Other Credentes begin to see glimpses of the hidden world, whether as shadows that lurk at the corner of the eye, or else auras and energy fields that are normally invisible to the naked eye. Others still experience momentary states of clairvoyance or heightened empathy, which can reach great distances. Increased health and vitality is very common, as is a new-found sense of nobility and confidence. Enemies who once seemed very menacing begin to appear small and insignificant, and the problems and stresses of their pre-Gnostic life seem to pale in comparison with the sense of endless potential that flows from the Gnosis.

Not all of the experiences are necessarily empowering immediately – some Credentes have experienced horrific visions and nightmares, others have experienced sudden misfortunate, or else ill health. Yet these negative experiences are often the result of the Holy Spirit burning away the spiritual cancers within the initiate, so that real growth can take place. It can be painful, certainly frightening. Yet tradition says that if the Credentes remain faithful to the Aeons, then they will eventually begin to feel sense of purpose or destiny, and a deep seated peace with their new state of being.

Over time, these brief strange occurrences begin to happen more frequently and with a greater sense of control. At this point, the Holy Spirit is well lodged within the heart of the newly awakening saint. The Credentes no longer fear the powers (called *charismas*), but learns to incorporate them into their daily life. Once the Credentes have learned to "dwell" within the powerful spiritual currents of the Cosmos, then the true powers begin to emerge. Tradition states that many saints gain access to powers of healing. Others are granted superhuman resilience to bodily harm, and are able withstand attacks or wounds that would cripple a normal human. Some saints are gifted with powerful physical strength, or else considerably enhanced intellect, even the ability to speak in foreign languages at a level that far exceeds their level of instruction. There are also historical and modern accounts of saints who are able to communicate with the spirit world, asking the archons and elementals for their assistance in protecting the needy, or else punishing the iniquitous.

These *charismas* are referred to as the gifts of the spirit, and many would-be Credentes have been tempted to join the movement, in hopes of developing these powers. This is understandable, but ultimately a sin against the Holy Spirit. The powers of the Void flow upward freely, seeking to embed themselves in the worthy – but they will not enter those who seek power for power's sake. Rather, the energies of the deepest of Aeons will only enter those who sincerely wish to become vessels for the will of Abraxas. As Christ says (Matthew 6:9-10) to his Nameless Father: *Your kingdom come, your will be done on earth, as in the Aeon* – which means, "may the Credentes themselves become your archons on earth, extending the direct rule of the Nameless powers into the Cosmos, and in defiance of the Elohim." The Aeons do not offer to teach the Credentes powers, but rather to make the Credentes into powerful beings. The distinction is subtle and yet important.

Perhaps one of the most power gifts of the spirit is the sense of meaning and direction which begins to develop within the Credentes. Many have turned to Gnosticism in search of purpose, feeling lost in a world that is bereft of meaning. Aside from the basic struggle to survive, what is the purpose of life? The psyche tells us that we are here to worship the Demiurge, and that our best hope is an externalized heaven where we will be frozen into an obscene parody of eternal worship. In this static heaven, the Demiurge promises to remove our free will so that we can no longer commit disobedience, or even free thought. Those less fortunate – who try to defy the psyche without taking adequate preparations to overcome the spiritual snares of the archons – they are doomed to a near-eternity in the hellish realms, which serve as the nightmarish prison-larder of the Demiurge and his agents, who devour the souls of the weak and wretched at their own pleasure. This is a horrid fate, which is to be avoided at all costs. After experiencing some bliss or torment at the Demiurge's whims, the psyche is cast back into the Cosmos and forced to take rebirth, unaware of its past lives, but born again to experience fear and degradation at the hands of the powers of Terra.

Yet in its infinite mercy, the Unnamable Father has preferred another fate for humanity. For those who choose here and now to partake in the divine essence, which is Gnosis, there is the chance of salvation. While the damned and asleep are curses to be reborn in ignorance and sorrow, the Credentes will ascend to one of two fates. The first of the two is the heavenly realms of the Pleroma, in which the Credentes maintain their sense of self. Within the Pleroma, they shall enjoy the direct presence of the Logos and the Lady, and will be given bodies of undying light. Little can be said about this heavenly place, because it is beyond all human ability to articulate by speech. Those holy saints who have fasted and prayed for years may achieve a glimpse of it, the vision of which is a great blessed. And still, this first blessing is the lesser of the two. For the second of the two fates is the greater, and this is convergence with Abraxas. For those Perfecti and holy ones who have undergone the sacraments and anointments, they shall not ascend into the Pleroma, but rather descend into the Void, where they shall achieve eternal union with Abraxas. There, they shall be reincorporated into eternity and infinity, which is beyond all hope and all despairs.

Convergence is, however, the ultimate fate of ALL beings. For just as Abraxas emanates the Holy Spirit, which emanates the Logos, from which ascend all aeons and archons, so too does Abraxas desire the return of all to itself. Of course, eventually ALL things will be reincorporated into Abraxas by force, for as the Christ taught (Matthew 24:35): *Heaven and earth will pass away, but my words will never pass away.* This means that even the aeons and archons, the Demiurge, the entire Cosmos and even the Pleroma will be pulled back down into the Void from which they emerged. Thereafter the cycle will begin again, except that the holy saints will never be parted from Abraxas again, unless by some mystery unknown to the Ecclesia and unspoken by Christ. Thus in Gnostic tradition, there is a profound different between those who seek convergence, actively making pilgrimage towards reunion with the Absolute and joyfully invite the slow process of Convergence during their mortal lives, as opposed to those others who (like the Demiurge) shall be utterly annihilated in the process at the end of days.

CONVERGENCE

Above we have explained that through the grace of the Sacraments, and through acts of Devotion and Austerity, the body can be made into a house for the Holy Spirit. This process is a sacred mystery, in which the human literally begins to be inhabited by holy energies and resonances which are alien to the Cosmos. This is not to say hostile to the Cosmos, but rather that the Holy Spirit is of a higher and older origin than the Cosmos, and is not subject to the rules of space and time. This is why those who are inhabited by the Holy Spirit tend to experience things which are normally outside the laws of nature (such as intuition) and are themselves a sort of nexus for energies which spill out into the Cosmos around them. Over time, a Credens becomes a vortex of spiritual energies from the Pleroma, which spill outside of the Credentes and begin to affect the environment around them. Credentes tend to attract the attention of elemental spirits and shades, because they radiate power on the spiritual planes. The Holy Christ is an idealized example of this, and when he encountered people possessed by lowly demiurgic spirits, they would react violently because they could see the aeonic energies within him, crying out (Luke 4:34): *Go away! What do you want with us, Jesus of*

Nazareth? Have you come to destroy us? We know who you are--the Holy One of God! The holy saints of various traditions have experienced similar reactions from those possessed by elemental spirits, which cannot tolerate genuine holiness. The Gospels also tell us that the Christ was inclined to send the spirits directly to the Father for remediation, but (Luke 8:31) *they begged Jesus repeatedly not to order them to go into the Void.* This is because they recognized that the Christ was an emanation of the Father, who is the Aeon, the very Spirit of Void, and the devourer of all spirits who are disobedient and wicked. By contrast with these lowly elementals, the Credentes pray daily to be sealed and consecrated so that they can experience the glory of the Father here now, and so that they will become a part of the holy Void while still present in the flesh.

As the Holy Spirit takes up residence within the Credentes, then, a fundamental change in consciousness begins to occur. The Spirit becomes the secret friend and lover, the inner voice which guides and protects. Through sacrificing the false independence of the soul, the Credentes are able to increasingly surrender to the control of the Holy Spirit, and become like Christ – and this is convergence. Now as lesser versions of Christ, the Credentes find that the world begins to become increasingly obedient to the Holy Spirit within them. Many saints have experienced the presence of the Holy Spirit like a gentle flame that simmers within the breast of the faithful. And where previously they experience mundane or spiritual problems and dangers, now they find that in particular situations, the Holy Spirit becomes suddenly awake, growing swiftly from a small flame to a raging tempest of fire which roars and rages around them. In such moments, the Credentes feel the Holy Spirit as if it is a caged animal inside them. It is no longer content to be dormant or silent, but an active and dynamic force inside of them, almost eager to shatter and remake the Cosmos around it. Thus convergence is an invitation to becoming part of the supernatural world, with all of the wonders and dangers which that implies.

This is *not* magic. Indeed, Gnosticism condemns magic as a selfish and dangerous practice, where very simple humans attempt to play with forces that are almost always entire magnitudes above them in the spiritual order. Magic involves the magician or witch usually (though not always) attempted to change the Cosmos so that it suits their own personal desires and ambitions. But the problem here is that is humans are not spiritually evolved enough to understand what complications or resonances such changes will make, or what the short term (not to speak of long term) ripple effects of magic will cause. Magical forces are very real, but most would-be magicians are similar to a child who plays with a loaded gun. With practice and some basic intelligence, the child can get the gun to fire – but the consequences can be very severe. Even in modern history, we have seen countless magicians, even masters, who have lead lives of quiet despair and even depression, despite their claims to command cosmic forces.

By contrast, the Credentes cultivates their relationship with the Holy Spirit (first), and with the other holy archons. The Holy Spirit is an internal force which, once invited in, will never depart. It can be dormant, but it can also be entirely overriding in cases where it wishes to direct the Credentes according to its fathomless will. If the Credentes allow the Spirit to govern them entirely, then they find that they have access to a terrible and divine force, which wants (fiercely) to be an active agent in their daily lives. As the Holy Scriptures say, (Romans 8:25-26): *In the same way, the Spirit helps us in our weakness. We do not know what we ought to pray for, but the Spirit himself intercedes for us through wordless groans. And he who searches our hearts knows the mind of the Spirit, because the Spirit intercedes for God's people in accordance with the will of God.* This means that even when we are not consciously aware of threats and dangers, or even opportunities, the Holy Spirit is aware, and is willingly and able to play an active role in steering us away from that which harms, or directing us to that which aids. This is not to say that life with the Holy Spirit is easy or pleasant, but that it will be deliberate and meaningful. When the Credentes are actively seeking convergence with the aeonic forces – that is, the Will of the Father, the Example of the Son, and the Power of the Spirit – then they are capable of wonderful and terrible things.

But it should be added that the Credentes are not expected to be merely passive observers, but to be assertive actors in their own plans and ambitions. We are not (and we were not created) to be robots. The Holy Christ says (Luke 11:9): *Ask and it will be given to you; seek and you will find; knock and the door will be opened to you.* This means that the Credentes should fast and pray diligently for those things which seem good to them, expecting that the Cosmos will be transformed according to their prayers, unless the Holy Spirit knows that the request is bad. A spiritual life, then, is a mix of personal hopes and dreams, directed by the Will of the Father, together with the urgings and whisperings of the Holy Spirit. Further, when we speak of the direction of the Holy Spirit and the Will of the Father, we are not speaking of the harsh and hateful moral impulses inflicted by the Demiurge – for these are the root causes of wars and crimes. The guidance of the Holy Spirit is often not given for "moral" choices, as the aeons are not concerned with human morality, which is a demiurgic construct. The aeons are unlikely to encourage truth or faith or loyalty as the Torah suggests it. In fact, the urges and impulses of the Holy Spirit are more akin to mad intuition and strange sudden impulses, rather than the chaste and shameful spiritual voices that seemed to haunt the medieval Christian monastics.

ECCLESIA MYSTERIA

A GNOSTIS DISCOURSE

✛

ECCLESIA MYSTERIA

A GNOSTIC DISCOURSE

Student: *Is there a God?*

Priest: Yes. Outside the cycles of time, there has existed in eternity a primordial entity, and all that exists has its source in His eternal being. The primordial being has always existed, and by its self-generating emanations it brought into being those holy Archons and Aeons who are the mothers and fathers of creation. In the tradition of some early Gnostics, this being is called the Nameless One. The Nameless is beyond all ability to describe – "it" is all being and all power and all glory. It is neither good nor evil, for it is beyond these things. The Nameless is not male or female or androgen, for It is beyond these things, yet according to sacred tradition Nameless reveals Itself as the Eternal Father. The Primordial Aeon is neither darkness nor light, neither hot nor cold, neither hard nor soft, for these words are too weak and too small to describe it. It is loving and cruel, caring and malicious, and it has the measure of the entire cosmos, for it is within each cell and atom. It is the final reconciliation and irreconcilable horror. The observance of His countenance brings both joy and madness. The name of each being, the number of stars in the heavens, and the secrets of the past and future are known to the Nameless One and to it alone. It is omniscient, omnipresent, and omnipotent.

Student: *Is the Nameless One called by other names?*

Priest: Different Gnostic and Hermetic schools referred to this primordial being by various names. Some texts use the name "Abraxas", others "Bythos" or "Autogenes", and others "Anthropos" – but these are generally titles rather than names.

Student: *Is the Nameless One good?*

Priest: "Good" as an idea has its source in the Nameless One, but Abraxas is likewise the source of the destructive and chaotic forces and beings sometimes called "evil" – as well those benevolent and caring forces and beings that people frequently call "good". It is better to say that Abraxas is *holy*, meaning that the Primordial Aeon is separate and other from us.

Student: *Is Abraxas a spirit?*

Priest: Abraxas is not a spirit, though it is the source of all spirits, which are emanations of its own primordial being, or else emanations of emanations (and so on) of its being. It is more correct to call Abraxas an *aeon* ('primordial deity'). Abraxas is not matter, though all matter exists as an extension of its emanations. The second member of the holy Trinity is sometimes called the Holy Spirit.

Student: *What is the Holy Spirit?*

Priest: Before time began, Abraxas generated the second aeon. This aeon is next to Abraxas in power and knowledge, differing primarily in terms function. In our branch of Gnostic tradition, She is called *Barberlo* the Holy Spirit, and She is the Eternal Mother of all aeons and archons. Barberlo is beyond genders, but She reveals herself mainly as feminine in character and is perceived sometimes as a goddess in some cultures. She is co-creatrix of all beings and is present throughout the visible and invisible worlds. Where Abraxas is present as the supreme emanating principle of existence, Barberlo is present as a dynamic force that permeates and influences that which exists.[1] She is the Spirit that proceeds from the Aeon of the Void.

Student: *Who is the Third member of the Trinity?*

Priest: By the power of Abraxas, Barberlo emanated a third aeon: Aberamentho the Eternal

---

[1] The Holy Spirit has been sometimes called *Ruha* (Aramaic: Spirit) and also *Qeryan-zan* (Iranian: The Lady Teacher). In recent memory, one recent British Gnostic attempted to summon a manifestation of *Qeryan'zan* (misspelled as "Koronzon"), and following the ritual, inscribed the name *Ba[r]balon* in the place where the Holy Spirit had manifested, thus indicating the connection between the two names.

Son. This aeon has descended twice in the flesh according to tradition: first as the Serpent in the Garden of Eden, then later as the Lord Jesus Christ. Together, these three aeons are outside the cycles of time and therefore co-eternal. This cannot be understood by logic alone, and is considered a Mystery. The Eternal Son is the aeon most concerned with humanity and with the material plane, and has descended into this world in flesh to teach and work signs and wonders.

Student: *Where is the Holy Trinity?*

Priest: On the one hand, the Holy Trinity are present in all places by their perfect knowledge and sight. Yet Tradition states that in their primordial state, they dwell in the holy realms of the Void and the Pleroma.

Student: *What is the Pleroma?*

Priest: The Pleroma is known by different names in many spiritual traditions as a perfect place or state-of-being, and in our tradition it is considered to be the Mystery at the heart of space and time. It has been called the Ocean of Light and the Shining Void. It is the ocean of colorless fire wherein Abraxas whirls as the maelstrom at its core. The Pleroma can sometimes be glimpsed in dreams and visions of blessed or fortunate individuals. It is the ultimate destination for the souls of the blessed dead, and is the original place of the Aeons and Archons.

Student: *What are the Aeons?*

Priest: The Aeons are the emanations of the Holy Trinity, cascading outwards within the Void. The Aeons are similar to the Father, Mother, and Son, save that each successive emanation brings with it increasing finitude. They are immortal and predate the universe, but they have a beginning in Time. The Aeons serve to make concrete the energies [themes?] of the Pleroma. They are perceived sometimes in nature as the laws and forces, such as time and gravity. The Aeons are responsible for the successive creation of the visible and invisible worlds within the cosmos. They are sustained by Abraxas and dependent on Him for their being. Most religious traditions do not encounter the aeons, for they are very far removed from the concerns of the mortal world. Instead, mundane affairs are more likely to fall within the realm of the Archons, their servants and helpers.

Student: *Who are the Archons?*

Priest: The Archons (rulers) are the emanations of the Aeons, whom mortals sometimes call 'divinities' or 'angels'. They are mighty yet more limited that the aeons, and so easier for mortal spirits to perceive. The Archons are dynamic spirits and active in the cosmos, where they have great power in the visible and invisible worlds. They were responsible for the creation and evolution of life within our own world. The

Archons possess free will and intelligence, and are of diverse temperaments and characters. Some are obedient to the Aeons from which they were created, while others are wilful and selfish.

Student: *Are the Archons the source of the world's many religious traditions?*

Priest: Yes, certainly. It is evidence that many peoples and cultures have unique experiences of the supernatural and spiritual worlds, and yet we can observe that their traditions are not always similar or consistent. This is because the Archons are disparate and willful, and some desired to be taken as gods and goddesses, where others are less interested in human attention or affection. The religious and national conflicts which we see today are sometimes the result of conflicts on the spiritual plane. This is to say that the Archons are powerful entities who are involved in the goings-on of the mundane world.

Student: *How are the Archons organized?*

Priest: Our tradition holds that the Archons do have their own society of sorts, organized in a hierarchical system that descends from the Holy Trinity. The medieval church's teaching on the angelic hierarchy is a borrowing from the original gnostic cosmology. Within the galaxy where Terra (Earth) is situated, each of the planets is ruled by its own Archon. The power of each Archon is strongest on its own world, but reflects onto the planets, just as the light of a candle is reflected onto the objects around the candle itself.

Student: *In this particular cosmology, where does the God of the Bible and the Quran fit in? Is "He" the same as Abraxas?*

Priest: No, not by any means. According to our gnostic tradition, the Elohim deity is a selfish and malevolent Archon which has undertaken to enslave and oppress the human species through a divide-and-conquer system of competing faiths. We note today how the Abrahamic communities are working to annihilate each other, rather to serve common goals. This is not accidental, rather, it is a design of the malignant entity which speaks through the Torah and the Quran. Both such texts allow divine sanction for such evils as slavery, gender inequity, and even genocide. No "good" deity would ever possibly desire such things, and so the gnostic tradition recognizes the Abrahamic deity as the great Enemy of the human race. We consider this archon to be "bent", that is to say, perverted from its original role in service to Abrasax. In many Gnostic traditions, the enemy is referred to as the Demiurge.

Student: *Is this Archon the creator of the universe?*

Priest: Not according to our branch of gnostic tradition, though the Demiurge may have been involved heavily with the shaping of the planet Earth, as well as with the evolution of our species. Here, we rely on the teachings of Christ, who refers to the Enemy as "the god of this world", meaning the Earth itself. Here, the Demiurge works to entrap souls in a cycle of perpetual reincarnation, where they are trapped in a false heaven, or in hellish realms of torment, or else forced to take rebirth again and again within the physical realm.

Student: *But isn't Christ a prophet from the Abrahamic system?*

Priest: The Christ Aeon took birth in Roman Judea among the Jewish people. However, a careful reading of the Gospels shows a stark contrast of his person with that of the Torah or Quran. Christ shows a disregard for the demiurgic religious laws, instead demonstrating a desire to help and heal the world, and a continued teaching that the Kingdom of God is not of this world. To the Jewish (later Muslim) teachers of his day, that was a blasphemy against the terrestrial-centered religious creed. Clearly, Christ was an inspired master who taught the basics of Gnostic practice, by which humanity is able to throw off the shackles of the Enemy and seek salvation through convergence with Abraxas. So successful was the early gnostic movement that it was only through a highly aggressive campaign by the Roman authorities that Gnosticism was suppressed and eventually the Catholic Church was taken control by administrators who corrupted the theology away from the original focus on the holy *Mysterium*.

Student: *What is the* Mysterium?

Priest: By *Mysterium*, we refer to the ultimate secret of the Pleroma which is only revealed through direct knowledge of that supreme reality. The process of gaining the Mystery is called *gnosis*, which means 'knowing'. By the mercy and grace of Abraxas and the higher aeons, a *gnostic* (knower) is able to internalize and incorporate the holy reality of the Pleroma, thereby transforming themselves into a higher being. This is necessary in order for humanity to overcome the tyranny of the Demiurge both in this world and in the afterlife.

Student: *What is the role of humanity in this cosmology?*

Priest: Regarding humanity, our tradition holds that we were given physical shape by the Demiurge, but were given souls and awareness of higher reality by the Holy Trinity. This myth is recounted from a demiurgic viewpoint in the Book of Genesis. Humanity is therefore a divine race, with its origins in the Pleroma. Christ teaches that our primary function on Earth is to become aware of our primordial origins, and to seek to return to Abraxas and the Pleroma. In other words, creation is a cycle of emanation and return to the source. This process of reunification is referred to in our tradition as *convergence*, meaning the act of deliberate reconnecting and assimilating. This is only possible through the miracle of gnosis.

Student: *What is gnosis?*

Priest: *Gnosis* is the direct knowledge or apprehension of the ultimate reality, that is, the Pleroma. Many of the world's spiritual traditions have a similar concept of "secret" knowledge which is reserved for very advanced adepts and masters. In our tradition, *gnosis* is a transformative knowledge, meaning that it changes the one who acquires it. It has been compared to a spiritual virus, which subtly shifts the mortal mind. Gnosis is salvatory in character, in that it saves or rescues the gnostic from the hostile power of the Demiurge. The one who gains gnosis becomes free from rebirth within the demiurgic physical or spiritual realms, and is able to seek rebirth within a higher aeon, or to converge with the Abraxas itself.

Student: *What are the effects of gnosis?*

Priest: Gnosis is powerful and transformative. It redeems the gnostic from the traps and snares of consciousness that are characteristic of the material world. By gnosis, the gnostic is able to "see" the material world clearly, and to pass through it as a traveler and not a prisoner.

Gnosis manifests in divers ways and at different moments in life. The presence of gnosis in a *mystes* (practitioner) should be evident in their day-to-day living, and be characterized by emotional and spiritual maturity and stability – which is not to be confused with cultural conformity. A *mystes*, more so a priest, bishop, or *perfectus*, should be distinguished by profound self-knowing.

Student: *How can we acquire gnosis?*

Priest: Through the grace of Abraxas, and by the action of the Holy Spirit, gnosis can be gained by mortals who follow the teachings of Christ. These are outlined in the classical Gnostic texts, many of which have been preserved faithfully in various manuscripts. Gnosis is of two types: *exoteric (outer) gnosis*, which can be communicated by sacred tradition and instruction; and *esoteric (internal) gnosis*, which cannot be communicated and must be experienced directly through the practice of devotion and the especially through the performance of the holy sacraments.

Student: *Is gnosis then entirely personal?*

Priest: General yes it is personal, insofar as the most genuine gnosis must be experienced directly and without intermediaries, though some exoteric gnosis can be taught via sacred tradition and study of the insights of the perfected saints and the Ecclesia (Church).

Student: *What is the* Ecclesia*?*

Priest: The *Ecclesia* is the Church, the Congregation and Community of the faithful who have seek the Pleroma. It serves to teach and promote the glories of the Mysterium, and to create the type of society in which gnosis can be more freely sought. The Ecclesia serves to offer those initiations which are transmitted primarily via apostolic succession. Finally, the Ecclesia also serves to offer the structure and guidance so that gnosis can be validated and understood in context.

Student: *Is that to say that gnosis can be invalid or misunderstood?*

Priest: Yes, and this is evident in the various mystic and occult traditions in the world today, which offer initiations and gnostic teachings of archontic (not Pleromic) derivation. For this reason the Ecclesia serves to offer guidance in distinguishing those revelations and experiences which flow genuinely from the Holy Trinity.

Student: *Is that to say that there are other esoteric paths?*

Priest: We can understand the other occult traditions may indeed bring the initiate into contact with archons and aeons, and thereby to obtain genuine spiritual insights. Yet not all archons are holy, and not all gnosis is nourishing.

Likewise, the hostile archons are capable of bestowing powers and counterfeit miracles on their disciples. Less dangerous but equally seductive are is the gnosis of those mysteries offered by those traditions which follow aeons and archons that lead to aeonic realms, rather than to the Pleroma.

Student: *What are the aeonic realms?*

Priest: As each of the aeons emanated in descending order, each created a realm as an expansion of their direct being. These are described as "heavenly" or "pure" lands in other traditions. Likewise, the hell realms of various traditions are likely the aeonic realms of malevolent emanations of the Demiurge. Our tradition holds that the souls of the deceased are forced to take rebirth in the aeonic realm with which they have the greatest resonance. For those fortunate souls who have undertaken acts of devotion within their own tradition, they may be able to take rebirth in a heavenly or pure aeon. Those who have committed sins within their own tradition may be pulled down (by the force of their own illusory guilt) into a hell realm.

Student: *Are the "heavenly" aeonic realms considered desirable within the Gnostic tradition as a post-mortem state?*

Priest: Yes, but only as a measure of last resort. The greater Gnostic tradition holds that convergence with the Holy Trinity in the Pleroma aeon is the ultimate desirable. Yet if the Gnostic cannot make sufficient progress in this lifetime, they may seek the protection and benediction of those holy aeons that are nearest in descent from the Holy Trinity. In this way, they may seek to take rebirth in a better aeon than this cosmic one in which we have currently taken rebirth. The Christ references this when he says "in my Father's house are many mansions" and later "I go to prepare a place for you, that where I am you may be also". If he were speaking of the Pleroma, there would be no preparation needed, but here he refers to the construction of a holy realm (aeon) for those simple souls who have good intention but lack gnosis.

Student: *You reference the term "holy" repeatedly. Is this to stress the moral goodness of the aeons and the Ecclesia?*

Priest: By no means, since "good" and "moral" are entirely demiurgic constructs that exist to trap the weary mortal soul. The Demiurge is clever in that it created mortal instincts, then provided religious traditions that run entirely contrary to those instincts – is this not the very definition of cruelty? It is evident from a study of the major religious texts that the Abrahamic and Dharmic deities are sadistic entities that exist to cause guilt and suffering, and thereby to entrap all but the most enlightened saints. And indeed, the death narratives of these major traditions usually depicts the majority of souls being dragged screaming to be tortured for having followed the natural and animalistic urges given by the Demiurge itself.

Student: *Is then Abraxas more kindly than the Demiurge?*

Priest: We have said earlier that Abraxas is holy, in the sense of "alien" or "other". So we should avoid Dharmic and Abrahamic systems of thought that encourage use to view the holy aeons and archons as tame or kindly beings. Abraxas is the very essence of infinity and eternity, so in a certain sense He has allowed for the demiurgic system to unfold. Abraxas and the Holy Trinity is ultimately pure in essence, but that includes all extremes of benevolence and malevolence in all their possible expressions and modes.

Student: *Then how is Gnosticism any better than Nihilism, if all souls are slaves to the demiurgic whims?*

Priest: Gnosis, as the Son, leads to freedom from fear and towards convergence with the object of terror itself. When one has become part of fear, then there is nothing to fear. When one has embraced ultimate joy, then there is no need to fear the ultimate torment, because through convergence with Pleroma, one has overcome and assimilated (thus mastered) these phenomena.

This is why the Serpent (that is, Christ) said to Eve: *if you eat of this tree, you shall not die, but rather become as the Elohim, knowing good and evil.* Then later, as Jesus, he says *Whoever believes shall have eternal life*, meaning that the one who believes in the gnosis taught by Christ shall have the true immortality, which is the Pleroma.

Student: *This teaching seems less comforting that what is said in the mosque or church.*

Priest: That is because in modern times, man has begun to think that religion is meant to offer comfort. That is stupidity, and a lie of the Demiurge. Religion is meant to offer truth and hope through direct knowledge of reality.

Student: *But shouldn't religion make the believer happy?*

Priest: If I cause you to understand that you are presently in trapped in a deep pit with a hungry lion, and that the only way out involves climbing up a rope of sharp brambles, will that make you happy?

Student: *No, it will cause me to panic.*

Priest: As it should, or else you would be mentally ill. But that fear is good and healthy, and it will force you to escape the lion, even though you may be cut and chaffed in doing so.

But having escaped, you will be free, and then warn others not to fall into the pit!

ECCLESIA MYSTERIA

THE BOOK OF PRACTICE

ECCLESIA MYSTERIA

THE BOOK OF PRACTICE

In keeping with the instructions of the Lord Christ, Gnostic practice is designed to create the conditions necessary for the initiate to (a) receive genuine gnosis, (b) obtain spiritual empowerments, and (c) enter into an ever-increasing Communion with the Holy Trinity. These three goals are intended to allow the initiate to become a vessel of the Holy Light while yet living, and thereafter to make the journey to the Pleroma (if fortunate) or the Void (if genuinely blessed).

Gnostic practices have always been incredibly wide-ranging. Unlike the practices of what has become mainstream Christianity, Gnostic spiritual technologies have always been intended to have tangible results in the material and spiritual planes. In other words, the basic practices of an Ecclesia initiate should show demonstrable effects within a short period of time, rather than taking months of years. If after several months of practices, an initiate finds no internal alchemical or spiritual changes, it may be necessary to do serious self-correction, and to consult with a senior member of the tradition for guidance.

There are three major categories of practices which are recognized within the Ecclesia Mysteria tradition. These are:

1. **The Devotions:** these are the practices which are carried out on a daily basis. They usually take the form of prayers and litanies, and are short enough to be memorized. These also include Austerities, which practices of spiritual and physical discipline. The Devotions are best put into practice as part of a daily scheduled worship routine. Most do not require a specific locale or *oratory*, and can be performed at any place or time.

2. **The Sacraments:** these are the holy rites and ceremonies which have passed down directly from the Lord Christ, and hence are considered to be direct conduits for the attraction and reception of divine gnosis. The Sacraments have been codified different and practiced in diverse ways by different Gnostic fathers and mothers, but they are generally in agreement on most of the rites (e.g. Baptism, Anointing, Holy Eucharist). Some of the Sacraments are described in this text in detail, so that initiates and potential initiates might have the opportunity to celebrate the Mysteries. The higher Sacraments, however, are only taught through personal (or apostolic) transmission, and require significant experience in order to be fully understood.

3. **Theurgy:** these are the rites and practices that are derived from the Hermetic

tradition, itself directly or indirectly inspired by the Gnostic communities of that age. Gnosticism views the Cosmos as a collection of physical and spiritual layers that interact and interlace. Thus we, as humans, are subject to supernatural forces against which we have little protection. Theurgy is the spiritual science by which the Gnostic initiate is able to counter those hostile forces, or to influence the Cosmos by inviting or directing ambient or benign aeonic or archonic energies to create a particular result in their material or spiritual milieu.

ON SOURCES

The practices of Ecclesia Mysteria are drawn from the rich traditions of the early Gnostic period, especially those of the Sethian branch of Gnosticism. These are recorded in three primary places:

1. **The Gnostic Gospels:** by the grace of Abraxas, many of these holy texts have been recovered from their hiding places in Nag Hammadi (Egypt) and the Near East. These texts cover a wide range of such Gnostic movements as the Valentinians, Basilideans, Sethians, and Ophites, as well as the holy writings of Mani and the Mandean communities.

2. **The Canonical Gospels:** these texts record the sayings and deeds of the Serpent-Logos, in his descending form as the Christ. The Gospels are reliable in terms of the sayings of Christ, however the recording authors had been coopted by the demiurgic tradition, and so these are read and adapted with caution.

3. **The Hermetic Corpus:** this groups of texts demonstrates heavy Gnostic imagery. Modern scholarship errs by trying to distinguish what is "Gnostic" or "Judaeo-Hellenistic" or "Hermetic", where in reality, the Hermetic framework was essentially a practical, flexible and cross-cultural system of Gnostic praxis.

Of course, since Gnostic tradition was never meant to be stagnant or frozen in time, and so our practices must be adapted by the classical ceremonies and rites, or else inspired by them. Authenticity – especially in the revival of ancient rites – can only adjudicated by intention and understanding of the spirit of the law, not the letter thereof. Hence we use and adapt the early litanies and practices as best as possible, and are otherwise unapologetic when modern times demand change.

DEVOTIONS

Traditionally, the Credentes should recite the Gnostic Creed each morning after waking. The repetition of the Creed serves to maintain spiritual connection to the Ecclesia, and also to fortify the Credentes against the psychic snares of the Demiurge.

THE GNOSTIC CREED

We believe in one Aeon, Abraxas,
the Lord, Father of all,
The God of the Void.
We believe in the One Spirit, Barberlo,
the Mother of life,
who proceeds from the Void.
She is The Light and all Light proceeds
from her.
With the Lord and the Logos she dwells
in Pleroma.
We believe in one Logos, the Christ,

the Serpent of God,
aeon from Aeon, Light from Light,
spirit from Spirit,
one in unity with the Mother
and Father.
Through him all things were made.
For our salvation he descended
from Pleroma:
by the power of the Holy Spirit
he was born of flesh, and became man.
He taught the mysteries; shed his skin,
then rose again.
He ascended into heaven and is seated
in glory.
His aeon shall have no end.
We believe in one holy gnostic
and apostolic Church.
We acknowledge one gnosis
for the salvation of souls.
We look for the Unity beyond Death,
Amen.

DEVOTIONS: PRAYERS & LITANIES

Prayer is a sacred practice which brings the Credens towards Unity with the divine beings. Over the centuries, saints of all spiritual disciplines who have devoted themselves to prayer have experienced rapture, ecstatic visions, and miraculous states of mental and spiritual revelation and perception. Our Ecclesia practices several prayers as part of daily practice, drawn from the classical Gnostic and Hermetic texts.[2] Devotion is a powerful tool, and prayer is one of the simplest yet most profound expressions of devotion. Through repetition of prayers, we align ourselves to the divine "frequencies". While the ultimate goal of Gnosticism is Unity with the Absolute Aeon (that is, Abraxas), there are many higher aeons that separate us from that supreme state of being. Thus Gnostic practice has been to work towards sequential ascension, where the Credens passes through the various aeons (or realms) in a journey towards the Absolute. For centuries, the following prayers have been held to be especially potent in terms of their spiritual resonance.

---

[2] The Ecclesia adapts several of the Prayers, Litanies and the Gnostic Mass in the following pages from the translations of Betz, H. D. et al. (1986) *The Greek Magical Papyri in Translation. Including the Demotic Texts.* University of Chicago Press.

The Credens should pray daily, and should commit these prayers to memory. They are especially potent in times of crisis. A longer form of prayer is the *Litany*. These are more challenging to memorize, but the process of memorization is itself a devotional act in itself.

THE LORD'S PRAYER

The Credens makes the sign of the aeonic cross.

The Credens shall say:

❖ Our Father, which is in the Void
   Hallowed is your name
   Your spirit come, your will be done
   On earth, as it is in your aeon.
   Give us this day your protection,
   And forgive us our failings,
   As we forgive those who fail us.
   And lead us not into folly,
   But deliver us from delusion.
   For your aeon is eternal.
   Amen.

AVE BARBERLO

The Credens makes the sign of the aeonic cross.

The Credens shall say:

❖ Hail, Barberlo, Mother of Light
The Aeon is with thee!
Blessed are you above all,
Blessed are the fruits of your womb.
Sovereign Queen,
Mistress of Pleroma,
Have Mercy on us.
Grant us your wisdom and your protection,
And deliver us to your kingdom.

THE LITANY OF THE *LOGOS*

The Credens makes the sign of the aeonic cross.

❖ O mighty Aeon, **LOGOS**,
Ruler of the realm
Above and master, god of gods,
O lord **ABERAMENTHOU**!

Celebrant again makes the sign of the aeonic cross (✠).

❖ O dark's disturber,
thunder's bringer, whirlwind,
Night-flasher,
breather-forth of hot and cold,
Shaker of rocks, wall-trembler,
boiler of the waves,
disturber of the sea's great depth,
I'm search with you the whole world,
Who finds the Demiurge,
whom I bring you chained.

I'm he who closes heaven's double
gates and puts to sleep that archon
which must not be seen,
Who stops the seas, the streams,
the river currents,
Wherever you rule this realm.
But as your soldier
I have been conquered by the gods,
I have been cast down because of
empty wrath.
Raise up your friend, I beg you, I
implore;
Thrown me not on the ground,
O lord of gods,

**AEMINAEBAROTHERRETHARABEANIM
EA!**

*Celebrant makes the sign of the
aeonic cross* (✠)

❖ Grant me holiness, I beg,
and give to me this favor,
So that, whensoever I tell
One of the archons to come,
he is seen coming
Swiftly to me in answer to my chants,
I have been attached

to your holy form.
I have been given power
by your holy name.
I have acquired your emanation
of the goods,
Lord, god of gods, master, aeon.

Then

❖ Amen, Amen, Amen.

THE LITANY OF THE AEON

(A Protective Prayer)

The Credentes make the sign of the aeonic cross.

❖ We call upon you who are in the empty air, you who are terrible, invisible, almighty, god of gods, you who cause destruction and desolation. We command your prophetic powers because We call upon your authoritative names to which you cannot refuse to listen:

**IO ERBETH, IO PAKERBETH
IO BOLCHOSETH, IO PATATHNAX
IO SORO, IO NEBOUTOSOUALETH
AKTIOPHI, ERESCHIGAL
ABERAMENTHOULERTHEXANAXETHRELU
OTHAMENERABA.**

Celebrant repeats the sign of the aeonic cross (✠)

❖ Thou are the Aeon, and we adore You. We call on your names, and let our cries into the Void.

[Address Petition here]

❖ For this reason We pray this prayer.

Then

❖ Amen, Amen, Amen.

ECCLESIA MYSTERIA

DEVOTIONS: HOLY AUSTERITIES

Authentic Gnostic tradition is very clear that the flesh is a divine gift, and should be celebrated rather than reviled. Traditions with hate and despise the flesh are deluded and self-destructive, and ultimately hopeless as we cannot hope to escape the flesh while we live. Further, as our branch of Gnostic tradition accepts the Cosmos as ultimately good and pure, we rejoice to be incarnate within it. At the same time, we recognize that the flesh can be disciplined, exercised, and perfected through various physical and spiritual practices. Many spiritual and religious traditions encourage a range of austerities which the masters of those traditions have used to great effect. Within the tradition of Ecclesia Mysteria, we encourage the health and fitness of all congregants, as there is much truth in the adage that a healthy body contributes to a healthy spirit. Likewise, our elders and spiritual forebears have taught that genuine spiritual evolution requires sacrifice on a physical level.

Credentes of the Ecclesia Mysteria are encouraged to undertake one or more of the following austerities on a weekly basis.

FASTING

The Lord Christ began his aeonic ministry with a month-long fast in the desert. Of course, fasting (in this context) does not always refer to an absolute abstention of food and water, but rather a severe reduction in the normal intact of food and water. Fasting has many benefits: (a) it helps purify the body, (b) it helps to discipline the appetites, and (c) it helps to attune the senses towards the spirit world. Many of the early Gnostic saints would fast several days a week as a regular practice, or else endure lengthy fasts of a month or more. Fasting is a powerful tool for the initiate, as it opens doors to the aeonic realms that will not open by other means. Credentes who make a regular practice of this devotion report frequent charismas as visions, dreams, and enhanced sensitivity to spiritual energies. The devotion of fasting is often done in combination with other devotions, as it has the characteristic of enhancing related practices.

HOW TO PRACTICE THE DEVOTION OF FASTING

There are several modes of fasting which the Credens may choose to implement. It is advised that new Credentes or those considering adopting Gnostic practice begin with the first fast (Bread and Water), and then attempt the harsher fasts after several weeks of practice. In order of increasing austerity, the fasts are:

1. *The Fast of Bread and Water*: in this devotion, the initiate reduces their daily intake of food and liquid. They may partake of three simple meals of grain and water – one meal before sunrise, one at noon, and the final meal after sunset. The initiate is encouraged to consume only a small amount of bread (2 pieces) or a small bowl of rice. It is permitted to take olive oil with the bread or rice for the morning and evening meal. In the Ecclesia Mysteria tradition, most initiates choose to fast one day a week. The fast can be undertaken for up to 30 days; to exceed this, according to tradition a Credens must consult with a Priest or Bishop.

2. *The Fast of Living Water*: in this devotion, the initiate must abstain entirely from food, and may consume only water. The intake of water is limited to three drinks: once before sunrise, once at noon, and once after sunset. This fast lasts for 24 hours (no more), though it can be performed twice a week.

3. *The Fast of the Spirit*: the most rigorous of fasts, in which the initiate spends the day in isolation and takes no sustenance or liquid of any kind. The day *must* be spent in prayer and meditation. This particular fast yields very powerful results, especially as a purifying exercise or a preparation for the work of the theurgist. This fast can only be undertaken for a 24 hour period (no more), though it can be performed twice a week.

Fasting is traditionally combined with prayer as means of enhancing the strength of the request. While the spiritual mechanics are not entirely known, the Ecclessia teaches that the austerity of fasting creates a sympathetic resonance within the Credens that reverberates very loudly on spiritual planes. For this reasons, spiritual figures who have dealt with spirits, like exorcists and shamans, have used fasting as a preliminary way of enhancing their personal currency with the spirit world.

In practical terms, a Credens may elect to undertake a fast with a specific goal in mind. This is not required by any means, but is a powerful way of attracting the direct attention of the holy ones. In this case, the Credens begins the fast with a short prayer that names the intention. It should be stressed that harsher austerities attract greater spiritual power.

As an example:

Jessica is a Deacon in her local Congregation. She has been harassed by a male colleague at work, and her efforts to seek meditation through the HR office have not gone well. She consults with a Priest, who recommends the Fast of the Living Water twice within the same week. Jessica decides to fast on Sunday and then Saturday. She begins the Fasting days with a prayers to the Aeons, asking for retribution and protection. Initially nothing happens, so Jessica performs the Fast of the Spirit a week later. The next day, the male colleague is in a serious accident and cannot return to work for several weeks. Jessica gives thanks to the holy aeons, knowing that the accident is a sign of her divine protectors.

✠

MORTIFICATION OF THE FLESH

In addition to fasting, one of the ancient practices common to many spirit-based traditions is the mortification of the flesh. "Mortification" is derived from Latin, meaning literally "to put to death", but figuratively meaning "to discipline the body for spiritual purposes". In a way, fasting is a type of mortification, since it denies the innate instincts of the body in order to enhance the spirit. Mortification is understood within Gnostic tradition as a type of self-sacrifice, where the body or its sensations are offered to the archons or aeons as a gift. This particular austerity is not an obligation, and some initiates may find it is beyond their level of faith or commitment. Yet those Credentes who have the strength to undertake the devotion of Mortification frequently are found to make considerably more rapid progress along the Aeonic path, accomplishing in months what others will accomplish in years. Mortification has many different forms and techniques, but several are particular to Gnostic tradition. These include:

1. *Chastity:* the practice of sexual abstinence is one of the most popular mortifications, and is found in many traditions. Simply put, the Gnostic must deliberately abstain from the sexual drive in all its forms – visual, autoerotic, or sexual play of any kind. The sensual instincts are not so

much suppressed as they are offered as a sacrifice to the Holy Trinity (or other aeon). The lengthier the length of the austerity, the greater sacrifice. It is customary for the celebrant of the austerity to mark the practice at its beginning with an oath. As example: "I swear by [name of Aeon] that I shall undertake the devotion of chastity for one week". Fulfilment of the oath brings satisfaction of the initiate, and is pleasing to the Aeon for which the austerity is undertaken. But failure to uphold the oath is a danger, as it is invites the disfavor of the aeon.

2. *Oblation:* the practice of sacrifice is another austerity which can be found in many esoteric paths. There are several different ways in which this austerity can be observed, though Gnosticism takes as its principal example the Oblation of the Lord Christ when he offered himself as the ultimate sacrament for his congregation. Gnosticism praises those who are able to emulate such spiritual fortitude, but modern times make such displays impractical. Thus in the modern form of the austerity, the practice of Oblation requires the initiate to offer a small quantity of their own blood in an offering bowl on the altar. This practice can be undertaken daily, provided that the Oblation is limited to a modest amount.

3. *Rectification:* The austerity of Regulation is the most challenging of the three austerities, and though it provides commensurate spiritual benefits. In Rectification, the initiate undergoes self-correction via self-directed corporal discipline. An example of this might include light chastisement (with a switch or belt), severe chastisement (with edged implements), scarification, and ritual tattooing. The discomfort is offered as a sacrifice to the Aeon or Trinity, and it is tradition to recite one or more litanies during the performance of the austerities. Rectification can be done daily, if the amount is limited in quantity. The second method is that of Rectification, in which the initiate scourges themselves with a belt (or similar device), and offers the discomfort as a sacrifice of sensation to the aeons or archons. During Rectification, it is customary to recite these lines from the Litany of Unseen Fire:

> *We call upon you, whose light is darkness, who shroud reasonable thoughts and breathe forth dark frenzy: clandestine one who secretly inhabits every soul. You engender an unseen fire, as you carry off every living thing without growing weary of torturing it, rather having with*

pleasure delighted in pain from the time when the world came into being. You also come and bring pain, who are sometimes reasonable, sometimes irrational, because of whom men dare beyond what is fitting and take refuge in your light which is darkness.

Like the devotion of Fasting, the devotion of Mortification is a very powerful tool for drawing down the attention of the aeons. As Mortification can be undertaken in different ways at the same time, a very driven initiate can use Mortification in conjunction with Fasting in order to achieve powerful states of gnosis or else as a catalyst for holy theurgy.

As an example:

Alex is Credens who has been practicing for four years, and is very devoted to the Holy Mother, Barbelo. He has been fasting and praying with fervor for some months, but has not experienced the kind of pneumatic ecstasy which he has heard other members of the Congregation discuss. After praying for guidance, he feels lead to attempt a week of intense austerities. During these seven days, Alex a) fasts on bread and water, b) performs Oblation daily, c) abstains from sexual contact with his partner and d) performs daily self-chastisement with 100 strokes from a knotted cord. On the final day of the week, Alex undergoes the Fast of the Spirit. During his day-long period of intense prayer, he enters a divine trance and enjoys the conjugal gnosis of Barbelo. Following his austerities, he returns to normal levels of eating and drinking. He shares his experience in confidence with a Priest, who validates it as a legitimate noetic experience.

DEVOTION: THE HOLY ROSARY

The Credens is encouraged to be mindful of the Holy Aeons at all moments of the day. One of the practices which has come down from antiquity is that of the holy rosary, in which the Credens recites the name of the aeons and archons in order to achieve resonance with their divine frequencies.

One might ask: why would this practice extend to the aeons beyond Abraxas? The simple answer is that the Supreme Being is so alien to this reality, that it may be easier (and safer) to engage in practices with those divine presences that are closer to Terra, and whom the great saints have had contact and communion with for years. The four holy aeons H*armozel, Oroiael, Davethai, Eleleth* are especially close to the Ecclesia Mysteria, and so Credentes are encouraged to perform the rosary in their honor. The Holy Queen, Barbelo, and the Serpent-Logos, Christ, are also exceptionally merciful, and so the Credentes are encouraged to spend time each day in prayer and meditation upon these holy beings.

In mechanical terms, the Credentes should secure a rosary (sometimes called "prayer beads"), which allows for keeping track of the number of repetitions performed. Many saints and mystics have reported that continued use of a particular rosary results in the aeonic energies saturating the rosary itself. In this way, the rosary can become a sort of talisman, which can be kept, or given to another in need of protection and benedition.

The pages which follow give several suggested rosaries that can be recited. Diligence in recitation is encouraged, and this practice is easily combined with the other Devotions in this handbook. Repetitions assume that the Credentes are using a rosary of 100 beads, thus one thousand repetitions is equivalent to ten cycles of the entire rosary.

The Rosary of the Abhorrent Countenance

To attain the benediction of the divine Abraxas, the Credentes shall say:

❖ Divinity of the Void
   Io Abrsax, Io Erbeth, Io Pakerbeth,
   Io Bolchoseth, Io Patathnax, Io Soro,
   Io Nebotosoualeth

(1000 times).

The Rosary of the Holy Trinity

To obtain the benediction of the Holy Trinity, the Credentes shall say:

❖ You are three: Wyrm, Wyrd, Word.
   You are Lord, Lady, Logos.
   You are the Holy Ones,
   And I adore you.

(1000 times)

✠

The Rosary of the Holy Wisdom

To attain the benediction of the divine Queen, the Credentes shall say:

❖ Ave Barbelo, Achamoth, Sophia.
   Have mercy and hear me.

(1000 times)

The Rosary of the Serpent

To attain the benediction of the divine Logos, the Credens shall say:

❖ Ave Aberamenthou,
   Ave Lerthexanos,
   Ave Christe, Ophis, Serpente,
   Have mercy, hear me.

(1000 times)

✠

The Rosary of the Holy Ones

To attain the benediction of the sacred aeons, the Credens shall say:

❖ Hail Harmozel, You are Grace, Form, Truth!
Hail Oroiael, You are Conception, Memory, Perception!
Hail Daveithai, you are Idea, Love, Understanding.
Hail Eleleth, you are Peace, Perfection, and Wisdom.

(1000 times)

The Rosary of Holy Seth

To attain the benediction of Seth, the Credens shall say:

❖ Seth, Savior, Proto-Parent.
Be present in our thoughts, words, and deeds,
In body, mind, and spirit.

(1000 times)

ECCLESIA MYSTERIA

THE SACRAMENTS

Sacraments are a particular ritual or ceremony that originates in the teachings and practice of the Logos, during his earthly mission. At first glance, these rites might appear outwardly simple – but in truth they are doorways to profound levels of gnosis. Weekly repetition of such sacraments as the Eucharist has a transformative effect on the initiates who celebrate them. Now the earliest Sethian Gnosticism traditionally recognizes two Sacraments are being of paramount importance: the Baptism of the Five Seals, and the Ritual of Ascent. In addition to these two ceremonies, the modern Ecclesia celebrates in addition several other rites that descend from the Valentinian lineage, these beings the Eucharist (or Mass), Chrism (Anointing), and Holy Orders.

ECCLESIA MYSTERIA

SACRAMENTS: BAPTISM OF THE FIVE SEALS

Baptism is a ritual that exists in many traditions and has complex layers of meaning. From an outsider's perspective, the ritual appears to be a simple bath, where the initiate is bathed (or bathes themselves) while certain liturgical passages are intoned. Gnostic tradition holds that Baptism is a major ritual, and in fact it is the primary initiatory rite by which a candidate for gnosis is inducted into the Ecclesia itself. It is a visible symbol to witnesses and the candidate of their passing from the state of being ritually dead to spiritually alive.

In the Ecclesia tradition, the ritual has five steps:

1. Preparation of the Candidate
2. Prayers and ululations over the Candidate
3. Five-fold Immersion in water
4. Investiture of glories
5. The Sealing of Five Seals.

In more specific terms, the Candidate begins the first stage (**Preparation**) with a rigorous self-examination. Have they, for example, considered the potential costs and dangers of joining the Ecclesia? Have they understood the basic tenets of Gnostic spirituality? Are they prepared for the potential spiritual upheavals that are likely to follow? Preparation also might entail the participation of a Congregation and Priest, if the Candidate is in contact with such parties. In this case, the Priest is responsible to offer advice and guidance before the ritual, and to help prepare the ritual.

The second stage (**Prayers and Ululations**) is the beginning of the Sacrament itself. The Candidate presents themselves wearing clothes that symbolize the old (dead) self, and the Congregation (or Candidate if they are alone) also has a cloth or towel (traditionally black) to cover the initiate in afterwards. The Candidate engages in an hour (or more) of silent prayer, and the Priest and congregants (if present) pray over the candidate. Glossolalia (ululations) may occur spontaneously, as tradition holds that the Holy Spirit can and does descend in force during this sacrament. The Candidate prayers that the Void will accept the offering of their psyche, in exchange for receiving the true pneuma. As one modern saint has written: Only those who sacrifice the soul can receive the spirit. The Candidate also inwardly renounces their birth name, and requests a new name from the deity in the Void.

The Third Stage (**Immersion**) requires five-fold complete immersions in water. This is ideally living water (lake, ocean, river), but any body of water will do. It is tradition for a Priest to bless the body of water before hand, but this is not necessary. At the head of each immersion, it is good for the presiding initiate to intone the names of the holy aeons as witnesses (i.e. Barbelo, Harmozel, Oroiael, Davethai, Eleleth) or otherwise names of the Nameless God (e.g. Erbeth, Pakerbeth, Bolchoseth, Patathnax, Soro). With each Immersion, the Candidate should envision the spirit passing through the various aeons so named.

The fourth Stage (**Investiture**) requires the Candidate to shed the old clothes (symbolic of the old life) and to be vested in the new should or costume. The Candidate receives a new name from the ranking cleric (or names themselves), and is crowned with a wreath or coronet.

The fifth stage (**Sealing of the Five Seals**) is the apex of the rite. The Priest (or Candidate) touches holy oil to the forehead of the Candidate five times, intoning the five blessings of Barbelo. The oil is applied in the shape of the Baptismal Sigil below. The Candidate should envision the seal being burned indelibly onto the spirit within. Thereafter the seals are understood to be visible on the astral or spiritual plane, as a mark of authority and belonging to the Nameless God. These seals are 1) foreknowledge, 2) incorruptibility, 3) life eternal and 4) truth, and 5) assuming the mantle of the aeon (Barbelo). These are necessary for the Rite of Ascent, which occurs later in the initiate's spiritual journey.

BAPTISMAL SIGIL

The Baptismal Sigil has an exoteric and an esoteric meanings to the congregation of the Ecclesia. Its exoteric significance is the mystery of the aeonic cross (or holy rood) on which the Serpent Logos suffered and died in order to share the Holy Spirit all humanity. Its secondary significance is as the eye of Abraxas, which sees all things. Thus the reception of the sigil is both the signing of the aeonic cross, but also the opening of the third eye, by which the Credentes are able to truly see the world through the unseeing eye of the Nameless Aeon.

SACRAMENTS:
THE RITE OF DESCENT

The Rite of Descent is a ritual that acts as a capstone to the other sacraments, and is celebrated only after one has achieved a certain level of gnosis and devotional practice. The Rite is intended as a catalyst which allows the Credens to undergo a moment of mystical unity (Gr. *henosis*) with the Supreme Being. Now while permanent convergence (Gr. *katastasis*) cannot be experienced until after death, this ancient Rite nevertheless allows the initiate to experience actual contact with the Aeon of Aeons, and to glimpse the great unseen, and to hear the ultimate silence. Though the Ritual itself is brief, if the proper preparations are not undertaken, such exposure to the ultimate spirit can cause madness and illness, even death. This is not a ceremony of evocation or invocation – since the Nameless God is already within and without us – but rather a ceremony of witnessing That Which Coils at the deepest part of the Gnostic's heart. For this reason, rather than ascending upwards or outwards, the Gnostic *descends* inwards, discovering the truth of the abhorrent countenance in the deepest parts of the pneumatic self. The text for this particular Rite is adapted from a Sethian liturgy in the Greek Magical Papyri.

PREPARATION FOR THE RITE

In order to undertake the Rite of Descent, the initiate should undergo rigorously self-examination and correction, in order to ensure that they are genuinely in a state of grace. It is advised that they consult with a Priest or Bishop as part of this process. The Rite requires several days of fasting prior to its celebration, in order to prepare the flesh and spirit to endure the strain of true divine contact. On the day of the Rite, the Initiate should bath and adorn themselves in their ceremonial garments, which should be clean and freshly washed.

Tradition states that the theurgist must prepare a small talisman (scroll), on which the theurgist writes the names of the four holy aeons (Harmozel, Oroiael, Davethai, Eleleth) as well as the names of the Holy Trinity (Aberamenthou, Barbelo, Abraxas). This must be done in ink mixed with the blood of the initiate.

The theurgist celebrates the Rite immediately after sunset, or alternately in the hour before sunrise. The hour before the Rite must be spent in prayer and intonation of litanies to sanctify the celebrant and the sanctuary.

THE PRELUDE

The Celebrant should offer a cup of strong wine to the Nameless One, which is consecrated then set aside. Then facing north, take the talisman, and touch it briefly to each of your temples. Recite the seven names (Harmozel, Oroiael, Davethai, Eleleth, Aberamenthou, Barbelo, Abraxas) then intone in a somber voice:

❖ = CELEBRANT

❖ Subject to me all archons and spirits, so that every spirit, whether heavenly or aerial or earthly or subterranean or terrestrial or aquatic, might be obedient to me and every enchantment and scourge which is from God.

The Celebrant shall make the sign of the Aeonic cross:

THE INVOCATION

❖ I invoke you, Headless One, who created earth and heaven, who created night and day, you who created light and darkness; you are Osoronophris whom none has ever seen; you are Iabas; you are Iapos; you have distinguished the just and the unjust; you have made female and male; you have revealed seed and fruits; you have made men love each other and hate each other. I call upon you, awesome and invisible god with an empty spirit, Holy Headless One, deliver me, **NN**, from the Demiurge which restrains me,

IO ADONAI ABRASAX AEOOY

❖ Mighty Headless One, deliver us, NN, from the Demiurge which restrains him (me) me. Deliver him (me), NN,

AOTH ABRAOTH BASYM ISAK SABAOTH IAO.

❖ He is the lord of the gods; he is the lord of the inhabited world; he is the one whom the winds fear; he is the one who made all things by the command of his voice.

❖ Lord, King, Master, Helper, save our souls, immediately, immediately! We call you:

IEOU PYR IOU PYR IAO IABO IOOW ABRASAX SABRIAM BYTHOS ADONAIE,

The initiate takes up the chalice. Saluting the north, the Credens drains the chalice entirely.

❖ Now I am becoming the headless daimon with my sight in my feet; I am] the mighty one who possesses the immortal fire; I am the truth who hates the fact that unjust deeds are done in the world; I am the one who makes the lightning flash and the thunder roll; I am the one whose sweat is the heavy rain which falls upon the earth that it might be inseminated; I am the one whose mouth bums completely; I am the one who begets and destroys; I am the Favor of the Aion; my name is a heart encircled by a serpent; come forth and follow.

Pause, then:

❖ I have risen, I have conquered, I have been anointed. The Spirit has descended upon me, and I have ascended into glory. Amen. Amen. Amen.

Having recited this litany, the celebrant should retreat to a quiet place and be open to the reception of visions which are likely to follow.

SACRAMENTS

THE GNOSTIC MASS SOLO CELEBRANT

FIRST PART OF THE OFFICE

The Celebrant shall make the sign of the Aeonic cross:

❖ = **CELEBRANT**

❖ In the name of the Father, and of the Son, and of the Holy Spirit.

Celebrant makes the sign of the aeonic cross.

❖ Oh Lord, allow us to celebrate the sacred mysteries. Let us confess our sins. Amen.

❖ Lord, have mercy.

Then

❖ Mother, have mercy.

Then

❖ Christ, have mercy.

Then

❖ Lord, take heed, and hear us. May almighty God have mercy on us, forgive us our sins, and bring us to everlasting life.

Then

❖ Let us pray.

FIRST INVOCATION

❖ **We** call upon you who are in the Void, terrible, invisible, almighty, god of gods, you who cause destruction and desolation. We call upon you, Nameless and Shapeless; we intone your hallowed names to which you will not refuse to listen: IO ERBETH, IO PAKERBETH, IO BOLCH-OSETH, IO PATATHNAX, IO SORO, IO NEBOUTOSOUALBTH. We invoke   you, ABERAMENTHOULERTHEXAN-AXETHRELUOTHAMENERABA.

The Celebrant shall make the sign of the Aeonic cross: ✚

❖ Holy Father, Sovereign of the Eternity, **Lord have mercy**.

Then

❖ Spirit, have mercy.

Then

❖ Logos, have mercy.

The Celebrant repeats the sign of the Aeonic cross: ✚

SECOND INVOCATION

❖ Let us pray:
Then

❖ **We** call upon you, author of all creation, who spread your own wings over the whole world, you, the unapproachable and unmeasurable who breathe into every soul life-giving reasoning, who fitted all things together by your power, firstborn, founder of the universe, golden-winged, whose light is darkness, who shroud reasonable thoughts and breathe forth dark frenzy: clandestine one who secretly inhabit every soul. **Lord, hear our prayer.**

Then

❖ **You** engender an unseen fire as you carry off every living thing without growing weary of torturing it, rather having with pleasure delighted in pain from the time when the world came into being. You also come and bring pain, who are sometimes reasonable, sometimes irrational, because of whom men dare beyond what is fitting and take refuge in your light which is darkness. Most headstrong, lawless, implacable, inexorable, invisible, bodiless, generator of frenzy: archer, torch-carrier, master of all living sensation and of everything clandestine, dispenser of forgetfulness, creator of silence, through whom the light and to whom the light travels, infantile when you have been engendered within the heart, wisest when you have succeeded. Lord, hear our prayer.

The Celebrant shall make the sign of the Aeonic cross: ✠

Then:

❖ We call upon you, unmoved by prayer, by your great name: (insert dread names) first-shining, night-shining, night rejoicing, night-engendering, Erbeth, Bolchoseth, you in the depth, Beriambebo, you in the sea, Mermergou, clandestine and wise, Adonai, Iao, Patathnax.

The Celebrant shall make the sign of the Aeonic cross: ✠
Then:

❖ Lord, hear our prayer; Holy Queen, hear our prayer; Holy Son, hear our prayer.

The Celebrant shall make the sign of the Aeonic cross: ✠

THE CREED

❖ The Aeons be with us. Let us profess our faith.

Then:

We believe in one Aeon, the Void,
the Lord Almighty,
Father of all that is seen and unseen.
We believe in the Holy Spirit, Barberlo,
the Mother of life, who proceeds from
the Void.
She is the Light and all Light proceeds
from her.

With the Lord and the Logos she dwells
in Pleroma.
We believe in one Logos, Christ,
the Serpent of God,
aeon from Aeon, Light from Light,
spirit from Spirit,
one in unity with the Mother and
Father.
Through him all things were made.
For our salvation he descended from
Pleroma:
by the power of the Holy Spirit
he was born of flesh, and became man.
He taught the mysteries;
suffered death, then rose again.
He ascended into heaven
and is seated with the Mother.
His aeon shall have no end.
We believe in one holy gnostic and
apostolic Church.
We acknowledge one gnosis for the
salvation of souls.
We look for the Unity beyond death,
Amen.

*The Celebrant shall make the sign of the
Aeonic cross:* ✠

THE OFFERING

[OFFERING OF THE BREAD)
The celebrant holds the bread in his hands,
saying:

Blessed are you, Aeon,
God of all creation.
Through your goodness we have
this bread to offer,
which earth has given
and human hands have made
It will become for us
the bread of life.

Then

❖ Blessed be God forever.

(OFFERING OF THE WINE)

The celebrant holds the bread in his hands,
saying:

Blessed are you, Aeon,
God of all creation.
Through your goodness we have

this wine to offer,
fruit of the vine
and work of human hands.
It will become our spiritual drink.

Then

❖ Blessed be God forever.

*The celebrant, before eating and drinking
the offerings, shall say:*

❖ May the gifts of Aeon be forever with us!

**While drinking from the cup, express
silently or audibly (if solo) your
petition, trusting that that the Cosmos
is obedient to the Spirit who hears you.**

The office of Abraxas (with or without
offering) is closed as such:

❖ Glory to the Wyrm, the Wyrd, the Word.
Glory to the Aeon of Aeons, glory
without measure, time without end.
Ending the acclamations as such:

❖ Thou art with us, O God Abraxas, and Thy name has been invoked on us, abandon us not O God Abraxas. We give thanks to you and we celebrate the eucharist, O Father, remembering for the sake of thy Son, Jesus Christ. Grant that we are always doing Your will through the name of Jesus Christ and will do Your will now and always. Make us complete in every spiritual gift and every purity. Glory be to You in the depths of space, time, and void.

The celebrant then says:

❖ Glory to thee, mighty Abraxas.

While making the sign of the Serpent's cross, drawing the sign of the cross: ✠

❖ May the Aeon sustain us always. The mass is ended.

SACRAMENTS

THE GNOSTIC MASS CONGREGATIONAL FORM

FIRST PART OF THE OFFICE

The Celebrant shall make the sign of the Aeonic cross:

❖ = **CELEBRANT**
▪ = **CONGREGATION**

GREETING:

The Celebrant says:

❖ In the name of the Father, and of the Son, and of the Holy Spirit. [All together make the sign of the aeonic cross.]

- Amen.

❖ The Lord be with you.

- And also with you.

❖ My brothers and sisters, to prepare ourselves to celebrate the sacred mysteries, let us confess our sins. Amen.

Then the Celebrant says:

Celebrant: Lord, have mercy.
All: Lord, have mercy.
Celebrant: Spirit, have mercy.
All: Spirit, have mercy.
Celebrant: Word, have mercy.
All: Word, have mercy.

Then the Celebrant says:

❖ Lord, take heed, and hear us.

- Lord, take heed and hear us.

Then the Celebrant says:

❖ May almighty God have mercy on us, forgive us our sins, and bring us to everlasting life.

▪ Amen.

Then the Celebrant says:

❖ Let us pray.

INVOCATION

❖ **We** call upon you who are in the Void, terrible, invisible, almighty, god of gods, you who cause destruction and desolation. We call upon you, Nameless and Shapeless; we intone your hallowed names to which you will not refuse to listen, *IO ERBETH, IO PAKERBETH, IO BOLCHOSETH, IO PATATHNAX, IO SORO, IO NEBOUTO-SOUALBTH.* We invoke you, *ABERAMENTHOULERTH-EXANAXETHRELUOTHAMENERABA.*
Holy Father, Sovereign of the Eternity, Lord have mercy.

▪ Lord have mercy.

❖ Spirit, have mercy.

▪ Spirit, have mercy.

❖ Logos, have mercy.

▪ Logos, have mercy.

SECOND INVOCATION

The Celebrant shall make the sign of the Aeonic cross: ✠

Then the Celebrant says:

❖ Let us pray:

❖ **We** call upon you, author of all creation, who spread your own wings over the whole world, you, the unapproachable and unmeasurable who breathe into every soul life-giving reasoning, who fitted all things together by your power, firstborn, founder of the universe, golden-winged, whose light is darkness, who shroud reasonable thoughts and breathe forth dark frenzy: clandestine one who secretly inhabit every soul. **Lord, hear our prayer.**

- Lord, hear our prayer.
- ❖ **Y**ou engender an unseen fire as you carry off every living thing without growing weary of torturing it, rather having with pleasure delighted in pain from the time when the world came into being. You also come and bring pain, who are sometimes reasonable, sometimes irrational, because of whom men dare beyond what is fitting and take refuge in your light which is darkness. Most headstrong, lawless, implacable, inexorable, invisible, bodiless, generator of frenzy: archer, torch-carrier, master of all living sensation and of everything clandestine, dispenser of forgetfulness, creator of silence, through whom the light and to whom the light travels, infantile when you have been engendered within the heart, wisest when you have succeeded. Lord, hear our prayer.

- Lord, hear our prayer.

❖ **We** call upon you, unmoved by prayer, by your great names: first-shining, night-shining, night rejoicing, night-engendering, Erbeth, Bolchoseth, you in the depth, Beriambebo, you in the sea, Mermergou, clandestine and wise, Adonai, Iao, Patathnax -- Lord, hear our prayer.

▪ Lord, hear our prayer.

❖ Holy Spirit, hear our prayer.

▪ Holy Spirit, hear our prayer.

❖ Holy Son, hear our prayer.

▪ Holy Son, hear our prayer.

THE CREED

CELEBRANT: The Aeons be with you.

All: And also with you.

❖ Let us profess our faith.

❖ We believe in one Aeon, the Void,
the Lord Almighty,
Father of all that is seen and unseen.
We believe in the Holy Spirit, Barberlo,
the Mother of life, who proceeds from
the Void.
She is the Light and all Light proceeds
from her.
With the Lord and the Logos she dwells
in Pleroma.
We believe in one Logos, the Christ,
the Serpent of God,
aeon from Aeon, Light from Light,
spirit from Spirit,
one in unity with the Mother and
Father.
Through him all things were made.
For our salvation he descended from
Pleroma:
by the power of the Holy Spirit
he was born of flesh, and became man.
He taught the mysteries; suffered
death,
then rose again.
He ascended into heaven,
and is seated with the Mother.
His aeon shall have no end.
We believe in one holy, gnostic,

and apostolic Church.
We acknowledge one gnosis
for the salvation of souls.
We look for the Unity beyond death,
Amen.

THE OFFERING

[OFFERING OF THE BREAD]

The Celebrant shall make the sign of the Aeonic cross: ☦

The celebrant holds the bread in his hands, saying:

❖ Blessed are you, Aeon,
God of all creation.
Through your goodness we have
this bread to offer,
which earth has given
and human hands have made
It will become for us
the bread of life.

▪ Blessed be God forever.

[OFFERING OF THE WINE]

The Celebrant shall make the sign of the Aeonic cross: ✠

The celebrant holds the bread in his hands, saying:

❖ Blessed are you, Aeon,
  God of all creation.
  Through your goodness we have
  this wine to offer,
  fruit of the vine
  and work of human hands.
  It will become our spiritual drink.

▪ Blessed be God forever.

The celebrant, before eating whatever is found on the paten and drinking from the chalice, before sharing the gifts with others, says:

❖ May the gifts of Aeon be forever with
  you!

While drinking from the cup, express silently or audibly (if solo) your petition,

*trusting that that the Cosmos is obedient to
the Spirit who hears you.*
[The office of Abraxas is closed as such]

Then the Celebrant says:

❖ Glory to the Wyrm, the Wyrd, the Word.
Glory to the Aeon of Aeons, glory
without measure, time without end.

Ending the acclamations as such:

❖ Thou art with us, O God Abraxas, and
Thy name has been invoked on us,
abandon us not O God Abraxas. We give
thanks to you and we celebrate the
eucharist, O Father, remembering for
the sake of thy Son, Jesus Christ.
Grant that we are always doing Your
will through the name of Jesus Christ
and will do Your will now and always.
Make us complete in every spiritual gift
and every purity. Glory be to You in the
depths of space, time, and void.

The celebrant then says:

❖ Glory to thee, mighty Abraxas.

- Glory to thee, now and forever.

While making the sign of the Serpent's cross, drawing the sign of the cross [✠], the celebrant says:

❖ May the Aeon sustain us always. The mass is ended.

SACRAMENTS

RITE OF ANOINTING

The Rite of Anointing is one of the oldest rites known to the Christian and Gnostic communities. Traditionally, it was performed for the recognition of champions and holy folk, though later it became a simple mark of divine favor. Since the Roman period, the Rite was performed for those of the faithful who are ill or dying, or else in need or spiritual fortification.

The Celebrant shall make the sign of the Aeonic cross [✠].

Then the Celebrant shall say to the petition:

❖ As our Father Seth anointed Grandfather Adam, So now I anoint your brow,

Celebrant dabs holy oily on the forehead of the petitioner,

❖ So now I anoint your limbs,

Celebrant dabs holy oily on the wrists of the petitioner,

❖ Accept now the grace and power of the Spirit, bringing you comfort and fortification in these difficult times. As oil burns from fire, so too will your spirit burn with the light of the aeons, which ends not but burns eternally within the Void.

GNOSTIC RITES OF THE ECCLESIA MYSTERIA

ECCLESIA MYSTERIA

CONSECRATION OF THE SANCTUARY

The Celebrant should select a safe and clean space to serve as a Sanctuary. If the Celebrant is a solo Credens in Hermitage, this need not be more than a shelf or cabinet; if a group of Credentes who have formed a Congregation, then a larger space will be needed. The Rite itself is very simple, as are most Gnostic rites.

PREPARATION

The Celebrant should place a basin of cold water on the table or shelf that serves as the altar of the Aeons. An image of Abraxas or other Aeons should be evident on the altar. A simple candle should be lit, and a brand of incense should be lit. NB. It is recommended to fast and pray on the day of Consecration.

Thereafter, the altar is considered consecrated, and should not be used for profane purposes. It is best if weekly, an Oblation is made as an offering to the genius loci of the Sanctuary. The altar should be kept clean and dusted (or washed) on a regular basis. The icons, candles, and implements of worship should likewise be kept clean and in good order. A Sanctuary is considered a liminal space, meaning that the aeonic energies are more vibrant there. It is good for austerities and devotions to be performed in

151

the Sanctuary, so that the Credens benefits from the spiritual energies of the place, and so as to maintain the flow of aeonic power in the site, which is activated through constant practice.

THE RITE

The Celebrant begins by entering the sanctuary and bowing low towards the altar of the Aeons.

The Celebrant shall make the sign of the Aeonic cross [✠] above the altar.

The incense should be taken in the right hand, and the four cardinal points should be censed.

The Celebrant shall bow to the altar again and recite the **Aeonic Creed**.

Thereafter, the Celebrant should say:

❖ Enter now, Nameless and Terrible One, this house made ready for you. For your servant calls and will not be denied. Enter now, Lady, this house made ready for you. For your servant calls and will not be denied. Enter now, Logos, this house made ready for you. For your servant calls and will not be denied. Enter now you holy ones, HARMOZEL, OROIAEL, DAVETHAI, ELELETH, and be at peace. Cast out all spirits and shades unfaithful to your holy names, and let this house be yours, and yours alone.

❖ Amen, Amen, Amen.

ECCLESIA MYSTERIA

CONSECRATION OF THE OIL

The Celebrant should place a small quantity of oil in a small bowl or jar, which is then place on the altar. The sign of the aeonic cross [✠] is made over the oil repeatedly while the following is repeated:

❖ In the holy names of Harmozel, Oroiael, Davethai, Eleleth, Amen.
  In the name of Christ,
  the Ophis, the Logos,
  Holy Aberamenthou, Amen.
  In the name of Barbelo,
  the Spirit, Sophia, Amen.
  In the name of Abrasax, terrible, silent, Amen.
  May this oil receive the blessing of the aeons, and may their holy essence empower it.
  This we pray, Amen.

Thereafter, the oil is considered blessed and has the charisma of blessing and empowering. It may be used for anointing of the sick and weak, as well as the healthy who wish for strengthening and protection. The oil should be kept within a Sanctuary and near the altar. It should not be exhibited before the profane, if this is possible.

THE HOUR OF RESPITE
(Benedictory)

When a Credens is near death, it is good for a Priest or other Credens to visit them. The Priest should make the sign of the aeonic cross [✠] and then anoint the patient with holy Oil, saying the following:

❖ Oh holy servant of the Aeons, blessed are you for your faith and perseverance. The Lord said: I go to prepare a place for you, that where I am, there you will be also. Be of good cheer and rejoice, for soon shall you travel to your true home. Be of good cheer, for soon you shall see as you are seen, and know as you are known. Ascend now in peace, protected by the Holy Spirit, and take your place in the celestial realms beyond. Amen. I bless you in the name of the Lord, the Lady, and the Logos, and the Terra, Pleroma, and Kenoma, Amen.

THE PRIMORDIAL ASSUMPTION

Within recorded Gnostic tradition, this rite is the supreme empowerment. It has been considered dangerous to perform, not because it brings bad luck, but because it constitutes a direct invitation of the Aeonic intervention in the celebrant's life. As the world functions largely under the machinery of the Elohim, this rite invites the Holy Spirit to suppress the psyche, and to bring the spirit (pneuma) into dominance over the consciousness (psyche), which can be very jarring for initiates of the gnostic mysteries. This ceremony was performed traditionally in order to bring Gnostic into alignment with the pneumatic self, so that one is constantly living as an empowered being, as an archon upon the earth itself.

Celebrants who have undergone this rite feel a dramatic increase in intuition, as the spirit becomes their constant companion and advisor. They become more attuned to those natural laws that govern fate and chance, and experience genuine Christ-like levels of tranquility, fortitude, and confidence.

This rite is appropriate for those initiates who, having practiced the gnostic path for some time, are grounded and stable enough to endure serious shocks which may come from the rite's celebration.

PREPARATION

The Credens should fast and pray the day before performing this particular ceremony. The ceremony is traditionally performed after sunset.

The altar should be adorned with a holy Aeonic seal, on top of which is placed a closed lantern (or a candle within a tall jar). Offerings of olive oil and ashes are poured into a ceremonial bowl, which rests on the altar. A chalice of red wine is also placed on the altar.

THE RITE

The celebrant begins by bowing towards the altar and lighting incense. Then then cense the altar and the four directions, and then proceed to raise the offering bowl to the four directions. Likewise, the chalice is shown to the four directions.

The celebrant dips their right thumb in the offering and anoints their forehead with the aeonic cross.

The celebrant prostrates before the altar, then kneels and makes the sign of the aeonic cross [✠] *and recites the following litany:*

❖ Oh, hear me!
  Abrasax, Abraxas,
  Abur-qad-Abur!
  Erbeth, Pakerbeth,
  Bolchoseth, Patathnax!

The Celebrant should prostrate here again.

❖ I invoke you, spirits, high and mighty, because you all knowledge and power flows from your realm, both the knowledge of the known, and the knowing of the knower.

Then

❖ Answer me, I ask you, so that you should be with me, so that you associate me to you by your power and virtues, that you fortify me by your aeonic essence, such that I can understand that which is secret, so that I know the unknown, so that I see the unseen.

159

Then

❖ Dispel my blindness and my shame, my folly and my weakness. Make me to climb the ladder of saints.

Then

❖ Transform my heart to be as the hearts of your saints.

Then

❖ Take from me that psyche which cripples and harms,

Then

❖ This is your blood, shed for the remission of guilt and weakness.

Then

❖ As the chalice was filled, I shall be filled by Your spirit. As I consume this, may I too be consumed by the will of the Lord.

The celebrant makes the sign of the aeonic cross over the chalice. The chalice is then drained. This ceremonial act is likely to cause intense feelings of dread and other strong emotion, which is healthy and normal. The celebrant should again prostrate towards the altar.

+ + +

This concludes the rite. Thereafter, the celebrant should withdraw to a solitary place and meditate on the gnosis which this ritual unlocks.

ECCLESIA MYSTERIA

ASSUMPTION OF ARCHONTIC MANTLE (LUNAR)

The Archon of the Lunar sphere is generally benevolent towards initiates, and is said to be of cold and humid resonance. Tradition states that Gnostics who have taken on Her mantle (gnostic empowerment) experience such benefits as increased wisdom, courage, eloquence, and good luck. The Lunar archon also bestows increased aptitude for research and investigation, for attracting sexual and romantic partners, and healthy fertility. This empowerment is very suitable to those who work in fields that demand public speaking, whether politicians, journalists, teachers, and administrators.

The traditional sigils for the Lunar archon are:

THE RITE

The Credens who wishes to assume the mantle of the Lunar archon should place the sigil of the archon on the altar, together with the implements of mass (chalice, bowl, etc). Then the celebrant begins by bowing towards the altar and lighting incense. Then then cense the altar and the four directions, and then proceed to raise the offering bowl to the four directions. Likewise, the chalice is shown to the four directions.

The celebrant dips their right thumb in the offering and anoints their forehead with the aeonic cross.

The celebrant prostrates before the altar, then kneels and makes the sign of the aeonic cross [✠] and recites the following litany:

❖ By the inexorable name of That which placed you over the sphere of Jupiter, we call you, great Archon. We call on you, given to cool thoughts and soft words, you in the heavens. Some call you Luna, or Chandra, or Mah, and others Qamar. We call you by your secret name, oh Lunar Archon! By the inexorable name and by these offerings we give to you, We ask you to resonate with us. Overshadow us with your gentle, silver glory. Oh great mistress, placed in a high aeon, cool and wise in nature, you are gentle and fair, the knower of secrets and senses. Aeon of loving and beautiful name, descend and dwell within us. If but for a while, descend, great archon, and deem to share the mortal frame with those who know.

The Celebrant should seat themselves on the ground and visualize the lunar power descending and filling them. The power should feel cool and refreshing, with and give the Celebrant a sense of mystery and gentle but powerful curiosity. For the next several days, their powers of intuition will be greatly enhanced.

ASSUMPTION OF ARCHONTIC MANTLE (SOLAR)

The Archon of the Solar sphere is of mixed temperament towards initiates, and He is said to be of hot and dry resonance. Tradition states that Gnostics who have taken on His mantle (gnostic empowerment) experience such benefits as heightened intelligence and wit, increased celebrity or rapid professional promotions. These favors are not without risk, as these advances tend to attract envy and bitterness from rivals (and even friends). The Solar archon also bestows increased aptitude for legal and commercial endeavors, and for dealing with people of power and influence. This empowerment is very suitable for those in challenging and energetic domains, such as executives, soldiers, police, physicians, and those involved in the legal profession.

The traditional sigils for the Solar archon are:

THE RITE

The Credens who wishes to assume the mantle of the Solar archon should place the sigil of the archon on the altar, together with the implements of the mass (chalice, bowl, etc). Then the celebrant begins by bowing towards the altar and lighting incense. Then then cense the altar and the four directions, and then proceed to raise the offering bowl to the four directions. Likewise, the chalice is shown to the four directions.

The celebrant dips their right thumb in the offering and anoints their forehead with the aeonic cross.

The celebrant prostrates before the altar, then kneels and makes the sign of the aeonic cross [✠] and recites the following litany:

❖ By the inexorable name of That which placed you over the sphere of Jupiter, we call you, great Archon. We call on you, given to cool thoughts and pleasant deeds, you in the heavens.

Some call you Sol, or Helios, or Surya , and others Shamash. We call you by your secret name, oh Solar Archon! By the inexorable name and by these offerings we give to you, we ask you to resonate with us. Overshadow us with your bright glory. Oh great master, placed in a high aeon, hot and dry in nature, you are glorious and life-giving, the sovereign of the heavens. You delight in generosity, so be generous to us. Those whom you love are blessed with good fortunate and nobility, because you are the source of noblesse. O Aeon of loving and beautiful name, descend and dwell within us. If but for a while, descend, great archon, and deem to share the mortal frame with those who know.

The Celebrant should seat themselves on the ground and visualize the solar power descending and filling them. The power should feel hot and vibrant, with and give the Celebrant a sense of courage and cheerful determination For the next several days, their confidence and leadership skills will excel.

ASSUMPTION OF ARCHONTIC MANTLE (MERCURY)

The Archon of Mercury is unpredictable in temperament, though generally not hostile, and is said to be of cold and humid resonance. Tradition states that Gnostics who have taken on His mantle (gnostic empowerment) experience such benefits as increased intelligence, memory, and wit. The archon of Mercury also bestows increased aptitude for the sciences, research and development, creative and artistic endeavors, subterfuge and intrigue, and for communication par excellence. This empowerment is very suitable for those in fields related to computers, information sciences, libraries, research and development, the sciences, and messengers.

The traditional sigils for the archon of Mercury are:

☿

THE RITE

The Credens who wishes to assume the mantle of the archon of Mercury should place the sigil of the archon on the altar, together with the implements of mass (chalice, bowl, etc). Then the celebrant begins by bowing towards the altar and lighting incense. Then then cense the altar and the four directions, and then proceed to raise the offering bowl to the four directions. Likewise, the chalice is shown to the four directions.

The celebrant dips their right thumb in the offering and anoints their forehead with the aeonic cross.

The celebrant prostrates before the altar, then kneels and makes the sign of the aeonic cross [✠] and recites the following litany:

❖ By the inexorable name of That which placed you over the sphere of Jupiter, we call you, great Archon. We call on you, given to cool thoughts and clever deeds, you in the fourth sphere. Some call you Mercury, or Hermes, or Budha, and others Hotarit. We call you by your secret name, oh Archon of Mercury! By the inexorable name and by these offerings we give to you, We ask you to resonate with us. Overshadow us with your piercing glory. Oh great master, placed in a high aeon, wise and clever in nature, you are the teacher of artifice and strategy, the swift of hand and wit. Aeon of loving and beautiful name, descend and dwell within us. If but for a while, descend, great archon, and deem to share the mortal frame with those who know.

The Celebrant should seat themselves on the ground and visualize the Mercurial power descending and filling them. The power should feel fluid and volatile. The Celebrant may find their powers of communication greatly enhanced, as well as their natural aptitude with media and technology of all kinds.

ASSUMPTION OF ARCHONTIC MANTLE (VENUS)

The Archon of Venus is generally benevolent towards initiates, and is said to be of cold and humid resonance. Tradition states that Gnostics who have taken on Her mantle (gnostic empowerment) experience such benefits as increased sexual and romantic prowess, as well as increased intuition and natural instinct for social currents. The archon of Venus also bestows increased aptitude for dealing with family issues, artistic projects, music, the arts, and fashion. This empowerment is very suitable for those who work in careers that involve charm and social skills, such as diplomacy, communications, fashion, and media.

The traditional sigils for Venus are:

THE RITE

The Credens who wishes to assume the mantle of the archon of Venus should place the sigil of the archon on the altar, together with the implements of mass (chalice, bowl, etc). Then the celebrant begins by bowing towards the altar and lighting incense. Then then cense the altar and the four directions, and then proceed to raise the offering bowl to the four directions. Likewise, the chalice is shown to the four directions.

The celebrant dips their right thumb in the offering and anoints their forehead with the aeonic cross.

The celebrant prostrates before the altar, then kneels and makes the sign of the aeonic cross [✠] and recites the following litany:

❖ By the inexorable name of That which placed you over the sphere of Jupiter, we call you, great Archon. We call on you, given to cool thoughts and pleasant deeds, you in the fourth

sphere.   Some call you Venus, or
Aphrodite, or Anahita, or Shukra, and
others Zohara.   We call you by your
secret name, oh Archon of Venus! By
the inexorable name and by these
offerings we give to you, We ask you to
resonate with us. Overshadow us with
your white, luminous glory. Oh great
mistress, placed in a high aeon, cool
and humid in nature, you are gentle
and fair, the mother of love and
guardian of affections. Aeon of loving
and beautiful name, descend and dwell
within us. If but for a while, descend,
great archon, and deem to share the
mortal frame with those who know.

*The Celebrant should seat themselves on
the ground and visualize the Venusian
power descending and filling them. The
power should warm and pleasant. For the
following days, the Celebrant will enjoy a
constant state of natural sensuality, not
necessarily (but frequently) manifesting in
sexual instinct ability. It is normal also to
feel enhanced compassion and affection for
friends and loved ones.*

ASSUMPTION OF ARCHONTIC MANTLE (MARS)

The Archon of Mars is generally inimical in temperament, and is said to be of hot and dry resonance. Tradition states that Gnostics who have taken on His mantle (gnostic empowerment) experience such benefits as increased vigor and energy, courage, and confidence. This archon also bestows increased aptitude for competition and conflict management in their many contemporary manifestations, be they legal, political, corporate, or social. This empowerment is very suitable for those who with careers in the police, military, the law, aggressive corporations, politics, and also for those who engage in competitive sports.

The traditional sigils for Mars are:

THE RITE

The Credens who wishes to assume the mantle of the archon of Mars should place the sigil of the archon on the altar, together with the implements of mass (chalice, bowl, etc). Then the celebrant begins by bowing towards the altar and lighting incense. Then then cense the altar and the four directions, and then proceed to raise the offering bowl to the four directions. Likewise, the chalice is shown to the four directions.

The celebrant dips their right thumb in the offering and anoints their forehead with the aeonic cross.

The celebrant prostrates before the altar, then kneels and makes the sign of the aeonic cross [✠] and recites the following litany:

❖ By the inexorable name of That which placed you over the sphere of Jupiter, we call you, great Archon. We call on you, given to rash thoughts and hot deeds, you who love bloodshed and hatred and harsh words, you in the fifth sphere. Some call you Mars, or Ares, or Bahram, or Mangala, and others Marech. We call you by your secret name, oh Archon of Mars! By the inexorable name and by these offerings we give to you, We ask you to resonate with us. Overshadow us with your red, furious glory. Oh great master, placed in a high aeon, warm and humid in nature, you are noble and fair, the kingmaker and father of rulership and noblesse. Aeon of violent name, descend and dwell within us. If but for a while, descend, great archon, and deem to share the mortal frame with those who know.

The Celebrant should seat themselves on the ground and visualize the Martian power descending and filling them. The power should feel hotly invigorating, and the Celebrant is likely to feel assertive, even aggressive. The power will manifest in competitive situations, allowing one to overcome obstacles and challengers alike. One should be cautious not to rashly engage in difficult situations that will outlast the influx of power.

ASSUMPTION OF ARCHONTIC MANTLE (JUPITER)

The Archon of Jupiter is generally benevolent in temperament, and is said to be of hot and humid resonance. Tradition states that Gnostics who have taken on His mantle (gnostic empowerment) experience such benefits as increased sense of honor, ethics, dignity, confidence, and good luck. The archon of Jupiter also bestows increased aptitude for diplomacy and negotiation, facility with bureaucracy and power structures, ability to lead and manage groups of people, and a facility with public, religious, social, and cultural currents. This empowerment is especially appropriate for people with careers in government, politics, leadership, and religion.

The traditional sigils for Jupiter are:

♃

THE RITE

The Credens who wishes to assume the mantle of the archon of Jupiter should place the sigil of the archon on the altar, together with the implements of mass (chalice, bowl, etc). Then the celebrant begins by bowing towards the altar and lighting incense. Then then cense the altar and the four directions, and then proceed to raise the offering bowl to the four directions. Likewise, the chalice is shown to the four directions.

The celebrant dips their right thumb in the offering and anoints their forehead with the aeonic cross.

The celebrant prostrates before the altar, then kneels and makes the sign of the aeonic cross [✠] and recites the following litany:

❖ By the inexorable name of That which placed you over the sphere of Jupiter, we call you, great Archon. We call you, given to warm thoughts and warm acts, you in the sixth sphere. Some call you

Jupiter, or Zeus, or Dyaus, and others Misteri. We call you by your secret name, oh Archon of Jupiter! By the inexorable name and by these offerings we give to you, We ask you to resonate with us. Overshadow me with your glory. Oh great master, placed in a high aeon, warm and humid in nature, you are noble and fair, the kingmaker and father of rulership and noblesse. Aeon of good name, descend and dwell within us. If but for a while, descend, great archon, and deem to share the mortal frame with those who know.

The Celebrant should seat themselves on the ground and visualize the Jupitrian power descending and filling them. The power should feel warm and regal. The Celebrant will feel a natural pride and sense of sovereignty. It is normal for the Celebrant to be naturally charismatic and grand in manner, and people will treat the bearer of the archon's mantle as if they are royalty. A sense of destiny and noblesse oblige often accompanies this sense of grandness.

ASSUMPTION OF ARCHONTIC MANTLE (SATURN)

The Archon of Saturn is generally malevolent in temperament, and is said to be of cold and dry resonance. Tradition states that Gnostics who have taken on His mantle (gnostic empowerment) experience such benefits as increased wisdom, sang-froid, resilience, and cunning. The archon of Saturn also bestows increased aptitude for intrigue, for uncovering hidden truths, finding lost treasures, destroying rivals, and keeping secrets. This empowerment is especially appropriate for people with careers in security, the intelligence industry, cyber-security, the occult, and information sciences.

The traditional sigils for Saturn are:

ħ

THE RITE

The Credens who wishes to assume the mantle of the archon of Saturn should place the sigil of the archon on the altar, together with the implements of mass (chalice, bowl, etc). Then the celebrant begins by bowing towards the altar and lighting incense. Then then cense the altar and the four directions, and then proceed to raise the offering bowl to the four directions. Likewise, the chalice is shown to the four directions.

The celebrant dips their right thumb in the offering and anoints their forehead with the aeonic cross.

The celebrant prostrates before the altar, then kneels and makes the sign of the aeonic cross [✠] and recites the following litany:

❖ By the inexorable name of That which placed you over the sphere of Saturn, we call you, great Archon. We call you, given to cold thoughts and colder acts, you in the seventh sphere. Some call you Saturn, or Keyvan, or or Zohal, or Chronos, and others Shani. We call you by your secret name, oh Archon of Saturn! By the inexorable name and by these offerings we give to you, We ask you to resonate with me. Overshadow me with your glory. Oh great master, placed in the highest realm, cold and dry in nature, you are noble and fair, just in your enmity with humanity. Oldest of the archons, first of the firstborn, descend and dwell within us. If but for a while, descend, great archon, and deem to share the mortal frame with those who know.

The Celebrant should seat themselves on the ground and visualize the Saturnian power descending and filling them. The power should feel cold and dark. The Celebrant will experience a natural sense of intrigue and facility with deception. Dark thoughts and grudges will rise to the surface of the mind, and the Celebrant will have many chances to cause injury to enemies. The Celebrant must take care to avoid being over-sensitive to offences during this time.

ECCLESIA MYSTERIA

CLASSICAL SETHIAN SCRIPTURES: A LECTIONARY

ECCLESIA MYSTERIA

AN INTRODUCTION

The early Gnostic communities of the Roman Empire left a considerable corpus of Gnostic scripture. Many of the early works were threatening to the Catholic Church, which made great efforts to suppress and destroy the Gnostic gospels whenever and wherever possible. However, by the grace of the Eternal Parent, some fragments and scrolls were hidden and preserved, to be discovered by archaeologists in the 20th century.

These texts are considered by the first Gnostics to be living and inspired words. While the human hands that wrote them were mortal, the will behind them was divine. Gnostic texts are empowered, and their reading opens the door to mental and spiritual states were it is possible to receive gnosis.

The following pages are an edited collection of classical gnostic texts, adapted from the original Coptic and Greek texts. They are best used in devotional readings and for recitation during religious services.

Before reading the Gnostic texts, it is customary to make the sign of the aeonic cross, and to pray that the Holy Spirit will open the minds and hearts of the reader.

ON THE NAMELESS AEON

The Nameless One is over all things, and nothing is beyond it. It is the Lord, the Source of All, Most Holy, Unseen and Unknown. No one can gaze upon it without experiencing death, so terrible is its purity of essence.

We should not call the One a deity, for it is the True Spirit, beyond any concept of deity. Nothing is beyond it, and it cannot be tamed or controlled. All that exists, exists within it, and it contains all things that exist and do not exist.

Alone, it is truly eternal, without beginning or end. It is perfect and without limitation, and so it has no needs or wants. It is the Power itself.

The Nameless One dwells at the heart of the Void, and it is the limitless Void. Science and reason cannot understand it, and there is no tool or science by which it can be examined. Eternal and undying, it existed, exists, and will exist without change or measure.

The Nameless One cannot be known [except by gnosis]. It is Nameless because it is beyond our ability to know it or call it by a name, for it is entirely beyond all naming and all knowing.

The Nameless One is absolute power, sanctity, holiness, and immaculate in its essence. It is without name and it is unknowable. It cannot sin or be sinned against. We do not call it good or evil or a god because it is entirely Alien and Beyond all such words. Our human words have no meaning for it, for it shatters and destroys those who attempt to know it [by reason]. It is not matter or immaterial, or big or small, and it is neither united or diverse in essence, for these are all primitive and small words for a terrible and dread entity. It does not have a father or mother or child, and it does not care about time and space, except that they are accidents that flow from it like the sunlight flows from the sun (without diminishing it). It alone knows itself, and no other one knows it at all. It is at the center of all, but it also contains all. Its power is perfect, and it knows itself through its perfect power.

The Nameless One is the core of sovereignty. All sovereignty and station flows from it, all governance and power, and there is no title except that it comes from the Nameless One. It is the source of every universe and world and aeons. It generates all power, all light, all life-begetting-life, all blessing and goodness, all knowledge, all wisdom. It is the power behind all goodness, charity, and mercy. It is measureless and unknowable.

The realm of the Nameless One is beyond space and time. It is stillness and silence. The Nameless One is the creator and preserver of all that is created, and sustains them through its limitless power.

The Nameless One is eternally quiescent, but it uttered the secret words: *zza zza zza.*

The Nameless One is being itself, true being, the only true being that is, and it alone exists without quality or qualifier. It is and Is Not, and it has within it all qualities and potential and paradox, though it is not defined by these things or limited by them. It is alien and unique. It is infinite and the essence of the Void. And in making, it does not lose and cannot be lessened or increased in any way. It is not a creature or like a creature. It is all Thought, and so it does not "think" like a creature. It does not have needs or wants like a creature, though it does cause things to happen and controls all events. It is more like a force than a being, in that it does not have wants or needs.

The Nameless God is beyond the deities and aeons, because they exist, where it does not exist or not-exist. It dwells in silence in the Void, where beings do not dwell.

It is not right to say that it is 'god' or 'holy' or 'good', because those are qualities, and the Nameless God does not have qualities. It possess something beyond all those qualities, and it is no word in human languages. It is not complete, but something entirely beyond completeness and fullness. It is alien and beyond and other, higher and above all the qualities of a god or aeon. Neither is it embodied or bodiless, nor large or small. It cannot be seen or heard or understood as one can understand a person or animal. It is unique, truly and utterly alone in its awful unity.

The knowledge of the Nameless One is the only knowledge that matters, and no one comprehends this mystery except it alone. It is not good to compare it to anything, because it is magnitudes beyond even the greatest of aeons. The archons and aeons do not begin to understand it, so great is its mystery.

It is self-generating and self-emanating and self-sustaining. It has neither wants or limitations in the ways that the aeons might have. Such things as completeness and goodness are proper to the aeons, but not to the Nameless One. It is in the Void, but it is also everywhere for everything that exists does so within it.

The Nameless One is great of countenance, and its face is veiled in mystery. All that exists has its being in the Nameless One, and the mysteries of the Nameless One are unknown except to it itself. Knowledge and Ignorance have no meaning when it comes to the Nameless One, as it is the ultimate secret in which all knowledge is meaningless. Abraxas is meaning and non-meaning together. The one who claims to "know" Abraxas has committed a terrible error, for Abraxas cannot be known or perceived or understood by the aeons or archons or mortals. Such a claim results in the death of the offender's spirit because the spirit is merely an extension of the Nameless One, and by sinning against the Nameless, the spirit is undone.

The Nameless God has countless eyes, but it is blind – that is, it does not see because there is Nothing to see apart from itself.

Nothing else is real, or was real, or can be real apart from it, and so it sees Nothing. It does not perceive because there is nothing to perceive. Yet it knows all things, especially its Mind (Ennoia) and its Son, the Logos, and through these things its knowledge extends outward and downward.

The Nameless God dwells in the Void, and the Void is terrible stillness and silence. There is Nothing in the Void, and within the Nothing is the Pleroma, and within the Pleroma is the Cosmos. The Cosmos cannot comprehend the Pleroma, and the Pleroma cannot comprehend the Void, but the Void contains them all and Abraxas is the Void. Abraxas cannot be understood. It does not "move" because it is omnipresent anyway. But through its Mind, the Holy Spirit, all things are moved by it. Abraxas is everywhere and always. It does not exist, because it is *being* itself. Likewise it has no being, because it is simultaneously Nothing. Abraxas has a form, but no matter by which a body is composed. Its being is non-being, and all creatures and beings exist inside of its being or as extensions of it. Now we are separate from it somehow, but through convergence everything will come back into perfect wholeness. Abraxas is incomprehensible, but we shall become Abraxas and then we shall understand all things and understand the Nothing also. Abraxas is in the infinite Void, and it is infinite and endless. From the Void, it emanated meaning and time and space and existence. All these things are inside of it, which is above them and alien to them all.

ON BARBELO

The Mind of the Nameless One manifested, emanating outward as the shadow if its glory. Barbelo appeared and stood before it in the depths of time and space. She appeared from the mind of proto-parent, before anything else existed, the source and cause of destiny. Her image is the reflection of the proto-parent's image, and Her light is the shadow of its light. She is complete and endowed with every charisma and grace. She is the literal energy of Abraxas, the invisible ghost, holy spirit, the first cause, the energy and vibration of the cosmos. She adores the proto-parent and is loyal to it, for She emanates from it.

Lo, the Divine Will! She is that which gives rise to every charisma and grace, and the Mother of all angels and archangels. All spirits of the Overworld and Underworld are subject to me, for they flow from me and have their being as a gift from me. She is within every spirit that moves and breathes and thinks, and She dwells within the living and quicken the dead.

She is the Holy Spirit, the hidden spring that nourishes all that lives. She alones knows the Nameless One, for She is the spirit of the Nameless One and its firstborn. She is within all things and She is all things, for all that exists does so as an extension of Her being, for She was there before the cosmos came into being. She is the whisperer in the darkness, the one who instructs about silence from within the silence. She is the quiet voice that speaks to the heart, full of wisdom and good counsel. She knows the silence, for She comes from the silence.

She went down into the darkness of the Abyss and revealed Her glory to those that were there. It was Her spirit that was over the dark waters of the abyss. She emanated all aeons and archons by Her thought, and She taught them their wisdom, powers, and virtues. Her true name is unknown. She is the source of all gnosis and wisdom, though She cannot be known [except by the wise]. She is the true Sound, speaking within all, and being perceived as She is part of the listener. She is the mind of the proto-parent. She knows about secret and eternal things, and She conveys understanding of mysteries which cannot be taught. She is self-revealing and self-evident to those who love Her.

She is the hidden grace, the secret charisma and bestows thought and mind and understanding. She is the great limitless mystery, inhabiting and empowering all things and beings. She is the unseen light, the hidden flame that guides the believer to those who live in the Pleroma realms.

ON HUMANITY

The Teacher said: Humanity comes from the primordial parent. The cosmos and its children is made out of thickening the light, which is the thickening of darkness (as diamonds as of coal). The powers have no authority over the Credentes, because of the Holy Spirit which dwells within them. This mystery brings eternal life to those who know it. Yet this mystery remains a secret, which lying dormant, awakens in future generations.

I asked: When will the secret become known?

The Teacher said: the Logos will reveal the secret when the time has come, according to the will of the Primordial Parent. Then the Holy Spirit, which is the spirit of truth, will reveal the mystery. The Logos will teach them about the Truth, and communicate to them the sacraments of baptism and anointing, which awaken in them the immortal essence. Being made immortal, death will have no claim on them, and they will enter the realms of undying light where the secret comes from.

On that day, the Demiurge will give up his dominion, and the angels and archons will bewail the consuming darkness. The people of the kingdom of light will know the secret, and they will see the Primordial Parent with their very eyes. They shall cry "Holy, holy, holy, we believe!"

FINAL WORDS

ECCLESIA MYSTERIA

ON JOINING THE ECCLESIA

Unlike many terrestrial churches and organizations, the Ecclesia Mysteria is independent of human authority, as its true heads is the Lord Christ, and the holy aeons and archons which have guided the Church since its inception. Having read this book, if you feel called to join the community, then you should take steps to do so. Seek baptisms of spirit and water, and invite the Holy Spirit to dwell within you. Pray and fast, sacrificing your flesh and soul to the Aeon of Aeons. Intone litanies, and sanctify your home and community.

One might ask: why the need to join the congregation? We answer that the Lord Christ taught his students that there is strength in numbers, and that we are stronger when working in collaboration with others of the community. When we pledge ourselves to the Ecclesia, we become part of something greater than ourselves, and become inheritors of a movement that is two thousand years old. Through the sacraments and austerities, the members of the Ecclesia take a share in all the blessings and prayers of the saints and archons, and experience a depth of protection and communion that simply has no equal outside the church.

The Ecclesia holds that there is no such thing as a self-initiating movement, because there is always a person or group that ultimately validates the initiations. But rather, we hold that true baptism and confirmation comes from communion with the Holy Spirit. Since we hold this as true, we invite all sincere seekers to join our community. To do so, simply pray and ask the Holy Spirit to enter you into the Ecclesia, and to connect you spiritually to our spiritual community. No other action needs to take place.

To say this differently: if one feels called to join the communion of the saints and to invite the Aeon of the Void to play an active role in their life, then it is that Aeon that gives the baptism, and the seals, and confirms them as part of the community. The Ecclesia is the body that results from that

Aeon's activity, rather than a group that invites people to join the Aeon.

But should you wish to contact the Ecclesia for further guidance, you may write to: ecclesia@safe-mail.net

ECCLESIA MYSTERIA

ECCLESIA MYSTERIA

www.ingramcontent.com/pod-product-compliance
Lightning Source LLC
Chambersburg PA
CBHW071337090426
42738CB00012B/2923